Reassessing Faith and Reason

Reassessing Faith and Reason

A Study of McCool, *Dei Filius*, and Lonergan

Jeffrey A. Allen

☙PICKWICK *Publications* • Eugene, Oregon

REASSESSING FAITH AND REASON
A Study of McCool, *Dei Filius*, and Lonergan

Copyright © 2026 Jeffrey A. Allen. All rights reserved. Except for brief quotations in critical publications or reviews, no part of this book may be reproduced in any manner without prior written permission from the publisher. Write: Permissions, Wipf and Stock Publishers, 199 W. 8th Ave., Suite 3, Eugene, OR 97401.

Pickwick Publications
An Imprint of Wipf and Stock Publishers
199 W. 8th Ave., Suite 3
Eugene, OR 97401

www.wipfandstock.com

PAPERBACK ISBN: 979-8-3852-5509-2
HARDCOVER ISBN: 979-8-3852-5510-8
EBOOK ISBN: 979-8-3852-5511-5

Cataloguing-in-Publication data:

Names: Allen, Jeffrey A., author.
Title: Reassessing faith and reason : a study of McCool, *Dei Filius*, and Lonergan / Jeffrey A. Allen.
Description: Eugene, OR : Pickwick Publications, 2026 | Includes bibliographical references.
Identifiers: ISBN 979-8-3852-5509-2 (paperback) | ISBN 979-8-3852-5510-8 (hardcover) | ISBN 979-8-3852-5511-5 (ebook)
Subjects: LCSH: Catholic Church—Doctrines. | Church controversies—Catholic Church. | McCool, Gerald A. | Lonergan, Bernard J. F—Criticism and interpretation. | Vatican Council (1st : 1869–1870 : Basilica di San Pietro in Vaticano). Constitutio dogmatica de fide catholica.
Classification: BX1795.C69 .A45 2026 (paperback) | BX1795.C69 (ebook)

VERSION NUMBER 02/05/26

Scripture quotations are from the New Revised Standard Version Bible: Catholic Edition, copyright © 1993 National Council of the Churches of Christ in the United States of America. Used by permission. All rights reserved worldwide.

Contents

Abbreviations | vii
Introduction | ix

1 McCool's Two Claims | 1
2 The Background of *Dei Filius* in Brief | 27
3 Faith and Reason in *Dei Filius* | 35
4 Lonergan on Natural Knowledge of God | 60
5 Lonergan on Acts That Lead to Faith | 86

Conclusion | 109
Bibliography | 111

Abbreviations

DB
: Denzinger, Henry [Heinrich]. *The Sources of Catholic Dogma*. Translated by Roy J. Deferrari from the 30th ed. of *Enchiridion Symbolorum*, revised by Karl Rahner. Repr., Fitzwilliam, NH: Loreto, 2002.

DS
: Denzinger, Heinrich. *Enchiridion Symbolorum*. Revised by Adolf Schönmetzer. 32nd ed. Freiburg: Herder, 1963.

HeyJ
: *Heythrop Journal*

HTR
: *Harvard Theological Review*

JES
: *Journal of Ecumenical Studies*

NIDOTTE
: *New International Dictionary of Old Testament Theology and Exegesis*. Edited by Willem A. VanGemeren. 5 vols. Grand Rapids: Zondervan, 1997.

TS
: *Theological Studies*

ZKT
: *Zeitschrift für katholische Theologie*

Introduction

THE TOPIC OF THE relationship between religious faith and human reason garnered widespread discussion in America in the middle of the aughts. It had already received some public discussion in 1998, when Pope John Paul II (d. 2005) issued an encyclical entitled *On the Relationship Between Faith and Reason* (incipit: *Fides et Ratio*). However, what launched the topic into the domains of talk radio, newspaper op-eds, and then-burgeoning social media was the appearance of three books that quickly became *New York Times* bestsellers: the paperback edition of Sam Harris's *The End of Faith* in 2005, Richard Dawkins's *The God Delusion* in 2006, and Christopher Hitchens's *God Is Not Great* in 2007. At the core of all three books was the view that religious faith is not compatible with human reason.

The popularity of the three books came as a surprise. While the mid-aughts are not numerically distant, the religious landscape of America differed significantly. In 2007, at the peak of the three books' popularity, the Pew Research Center surveyed 35,000 American adults via telephone on the topic of religion. Of interest here are the statistics for so-called religious "nones": atheists stood at 1.6 percent, agnostics at 2.4 percent, and "nothing in particular" persons at 12.1 percent.[1] Given these statistics, one would expect some interest in Harris, Dawkins, and Hitchens, but not a

---

1. Gregory Smith, "Changing Religious Composition," para. 25.

INTRODUCTION

year-after-year achievement of bestseller status. The character of the religious landscape can also be gleaned from the literary response to the books. Less than a year after Hitchens's book was published, Timothy Keller's *The Reason for God*, which challenged claims made in all three books, itself became a *New York Times* bestseller.

In 2014, Pew again surveyed 35,000 American adults to find out what, if anything, had changed since 2007. The data revealed a substantial increase in religious "nones": atheists had grown to 3.1 percent, agnostics had grown to 4.0 percent, and "nothing in particular" persons had grown to 15.8 percent.[2] The doubling of atheists and near-doubling of agnostics led Pew to remark in its report, "The 'nones' appear to be growing more secular." Even within the "nothing in particular" group, where some persons still find religion (in general) to be meaningful in their lives, it was the share deeming religion "unimportant" that grew the most. It was at this point that a societal shift could be felt, wherein the bestseller status of *The End of Faith*, *The God Delusion*, and *God Is Not Great* did not conjure the same sense of surprise that it did seven years prior. Clearly there was some overlap between the views of the "nones" and the views presented in the three books; determining the extent of the overlap would require additional surveying.

In 2016, Pew shared the results of a new survey, in which they contacted 5,000 of the 35,000 adults previously interviewed.[3] Pew wanted to find out, among other things, *why* "nones" are "nones." Of note here is the share of "nones" who were raised in a religion but now claimed to be atheist, agnostic, or "nothing in particular."[4] When asked why this was so, the most common response (49 percent) was a lack of belief.[5] With respect to the source of the lack of belief, "sci-

---

2. Gregory Smith, "Changing Religious Composition," para. 25.

3. For an overview of the survey, see Lipka, "America's 'Nones.'"

4. "The vast majority of . . . 'nones' (78 percent) say they were raised as a member of a particular religion before shedding their religious identity in adulthood" (Lipka, "America's 'Nones,'" para. 1).

5. Lipka, "America's 'Nones,'" para. 3. Other bases for leaving included a dislike of organized religion (20 percent), a desire to remain open (18 percent), and religious inactivity (10 percent) (paras. 4–6).

Introduction

ence" was invoked most frequently; other sources included "common sense," "logic," and "a lack of evidence." For practical purposes, these sources will henceforth be referred to using one term: *reason*. Plainly, the change of aura around the three books' bestseller status was strongly linked to their echoing of a view—that religious faith is not compatible with human reason—now held by about 10 percent of the American adult population.[6] It would be imprudent, though, to assume the three books to be completely representational of this group without further surveying.

In 2018, Pew shared the results of a smaller-scale survey that sought to ascertain whether "nones," despite having abandoned *religious faith* (Judaism, Christianity, Islam, and so forth), continue to believe in the existence of God "as described in the Bible" or as "a higher power or spiritual force." The results showed that no atheists and only 3 percent of agnostics claim to believe that God, "as described in the Bible," exists.[7] On this point, the two groups align with *The End of Faith*, *The God Delusion*, and *God Is Not Great*. However, the three books also uphold skepticism about the supernatural in general. It is here that a caveat is required regarding their status as representative of the "nones," for according to Pew, 18 percent of atheists and 62 percent of agnostics believe that "a higher power or spiritual force" exists.[8] The caveat is not so great, however, as to make the changed aura of the books a mystery. Even among "nothing in particular" persons, of whom 60 percent believe that "a higher power or spiritual force" exists and 28 percent that God, "as described in the Bible," exists, the most common basis for not identifying with a religious faith was *reason*.

At the time of writing, Pew has not yet conducted a survey on religion that meets the scale of those done in 2007 and 2014. However, a smaller 2021 survey, not focused exclusively on

---

6. This is an inference. The three subgroups of "nones" noted above totalled 22 percent of American adults in 2014. Among the "nones" who did identify with a religion but ceased (78 percent of "nones"), half ceased on the basis of reason, and just under half of 22 percent is 10 percent.

7. Cooperman et al., *Americans Say They Believe*, paras. 24–25.

8. Cooperman et al., *Americans Say They Believe*, paras. 24–25.

Introduction

religion and not conducted via telephone, found that atheists stand at 4 percent, agnostics at 5 percent, and "nothing in particular" persons at 20 percent.[9] The article containing the data concludes, "The secularizing shifts evident in American society so far in the twenty-first century show no signs of slowing." One can infer from this that reason-based departure from religious faith will grow in the coming years, including reason-based departure from belief in God, as described in the Bible, and from belief in a higher power or spiritual force.

* * *

This book is a response to the phenomenon detailed above. In sum, the phenomenon is the entrance into public conversation and subsequent growth of the view that religious faith is not compatible with human reason. Importantly, it is the phenomenon that is being responded to, not the case made for the incompatibility of faith and reason found in *The End of Faith*, *The God Delusion*, and *God Is Not Great*. That case now has wide acceptance, under the guise of bases such as "science," "common sense," "logic," and "a lack of evidence." When a view shifts from outlier to mainstream, a scholar who disagrees with it should refrain from defense and instead reassess the articulation found in his or her own tradition—in this case, the articulation of the relationship between religious faith and human reason. Needless to say, this undertaking will differ from one religious tradition to the next. In this book, the articulation in the Roman Catholic tradition will be reassessed. Here, "reassess" means to explore a matter with a heightened expectation of clarity and to give attention to its under-investigated aspects. These attitudes, which are normally avoided for their potential damage to the integrity of tradition, take on the status of public service when a view changes from outlier to mainstream.

---

9. Gregory Smith, "About Three-in-Ten U.S. Adults." Within the "nothing in particular" group, 78 percent deem religion "not too or not at all important in their lives."

INTRODUCTION

Where does one cast one's attention to reassess the articulation of the relationship between faith and reason in the Roman Catholic tradition? On first reflection, it seems plain that the answer is Pope John Paul II's *Fides et Ratio*. It is a recent text of high authority whose title could not be more relevant. Despite that, as one reads the text the necessity of digging deeper comes to light. One passage is especially indicative of this need. Discussing the springing up of several magisterial documents pertaining to faith and reason in the 1800s, Pope John Paul II writes,

> In that period not a few Catholics felt it their duty to counter various streams of modern thought with a philosophy of their own. At this point, the Magisterium of the Church was obliged to be vigilant lest these philosophies developed in ways which were themselves erroneous and negative. The censures were delivered even-handedly: on the one hand, *fideism* and *radical traditionalism*, for their distrust of reason's natural capacities, and, on the other, *rationalism* and *ontologism* because they attributed to natural reason a knowledge which only the light of faith could confer. The positive elements of this debate were assembled in the Dogmatic Constitution *Dei Filius*, in which for the first time an Ecumenical Council—in this case, the First Vatican Council—pronounced solemnly on the relationship between reason and faith. The teaching contained in this document strongly and positively marked the philosophical research of many believers and remains today a standard reference-point for correct and coherent Christian thinking in this regard.[10]

This passage designates another, older document as a reference-point for thinking about faith and reason: the *Dogmatic Constitution on the Catholic Faith* (incipit: *Dei Filius*). Indeed, as Avery Dulles states, "The official Catholic position [on the relationship between faith and reason] was most authoritatively summarized in 1870 by the First Vatican Council in its *Dogmatic Constitution*."[11]

10. John Paul II, *Fides et Ratio*, 69–70, §52; emphasis in original.

11. Dulles, "Faith and Reason," 193. On the authority of dogmatic constitutions, such as *Dei Filius*, see Congregation for the Doctrine of the Faith, "Commentary on *Professio Fidei*"; Gaillardetz, "What the Church Teaches."

INTRODUCTION

Fides et Ratio, it should be noted, is not the only magisterial document to convey the reference-point status of *Dei Filius*.[12] The Second Vatican Council's *Dogmatic Constitution on Divine Revelation* (incipit: *Dei Verbum*) states that it is "following . . . in the steps of the Councils of Trent and Vatican I."[13] And the document goes on to make eight references to *Dei Filius* in its notes. A more recent document that makes recourse to *Dei Filius* is the 2013 encyclical *Lumen Fidei*, issued by Pope Francis (d. 2025). Pope Francis states that he is writing "in continuity with all that the Church's magisterium has pronounced on this theological virtue [namely, faith]," and he attaches a note to this statement that refers to *Dei Filius*.[14]

Some persons might wonder why the *Catechism of the Catholic Church* cannot serve as a focal text in the project of reassessment, especially in light of one of Pope John Paul II's remarks about it. In the 1992 document in which he promulgates the catechism, he writes, "I declare it to be a valid and legitimate instrument for ecclesial communion and a sure norm for teaching the faith."[15] And the catechism does indeed refer to the statement about natural knowledge of God in *Dei Filius*. Nonetheless, the catechism employs an expression not found in *Dei Filius*; it speaks of proofs for the existence of God "in the sense of 'converging and convincing arguments.'"[16] Moreover, the catechism quotes all of

---

12. For a summary of references made to *Dei Filius* in *Fides et Ratio*, see Dulles, "Faith and Reason," 195.

13. Second Vatican Council, *Dei Verbum*, 750, §1.

14. The note he attaches to this statement contains a reference to the third chapter of *Dei Filius*. See Francis, *Lumen Fidei*, 10n7, §7.

15. John Paul II, *Fidei Depositum*, §4.

16. Catholic Church, *Catechism*, 14–15, §31. The expression recalls—but gives no indication of referring to—Newman's idea of "the cumulation of probabilities, independent of each other, arising out of the nature and circumstances of the particular case which is under review; probabilities too fine to avail separately, too subtle and circuitous to be convertible into syllogisms, too numerous and various for such conversion" (Newman, *Grammar of Assent* 8.2).

INTRODUCTION

Rom 1:19–20, whereas *Dei Filius* quotes only part of Rom 1:20.[17] These sorts of divergences render the catechism unsuitable as a focal text in this book's project of reassessment, as does the following statement by Joseph Ratzinger (before being elected pope): "The individual doctrines which the *Catechism* presents receive no other weight than that which they already possess."[18]

* * *

Having isolated *Dei Filius* as the locus of the standard articulation of the relationship between religious faith and human reason in Roman Catholicism, an examination of it is an appealing way to start this book. However, the project of reassessment involves a commitment to not leave stones unturned. As the passage from *Fides et Ratio* above relays, a debate about the relationship between faith and reason is what provoked the composition of *Dei Filius*— and this must be explored first, even though *Dei Filius* formally ended the debate.

A great debt is owed to Gerald McCool[19] for providing an overview of the debate in *Nineteenth-Century Scholasticism: The Search for a Unitary Method*, first published in 1977.[20] In the course of the overview, McCool makes two surprising claims. Delving into these two claims is one of this book's contributions to the project of reassessment.

To explain McCool's two claims, it is helpful to return to the lengthy passage above from *Fides et Ratio*. Pope John Paul II attaches a footnote to each of the four positions he identifies. The footnote attached to *fideism* references a censure of the Roman Catholic thinker Louis Bautain; the footnote attached to

17. Catholic Church, *Catechism*, 15, §32.
18. Ratzinger, "Author of the Catechism," 26; emphasis added.
19. McCool obtained a PhD in philosophy from Fordham University in 1956. He served as a faculty member there for several decades and authored many books and articles. He passed away July 26, 2005.
20. The 1977 publication is entitled *Catholic Theology in the Nineteenth Century: The Quest for a Unitary Method*. The pagination is identical.

INTRODUCTION

rationalism references a censure of the Roman Catholic thinker Anton Günther.[21] And Pope John Paul II places these positions on opposing sides of the debate about the relationship between faith and reason. It comes as a surprise, then, to read McCool's claim that Bautain and Günther appropriated the same epistemology. It also comes as a surprise to read McCool's claim that Joseph Kleutgen, the main author of *Dei Filius*, engaged in an attack on this epistemology years before the First Vatican Council. Plainly, McCool's two claims, and the connection between them, have the prospect of unveiling additional layers of *Dei Filius*. Chapter 1 of this book assesses the two claims.

It goes without saying that there are additional dimensions of the debate that provoked *Dei Filius*. In footnotes attached to the lengthy passage from *Fides et Ratio*, references are made to censures of other theologians involved in the debate about the relationship between faith and reason.[22] Furthermore, in *Nineteenth-Century Scholasticism*, McCool finds other theologians wedded to the epistemology that Bautain and Günther appropriated.[23] This raises the question as to why this book attends not just to one dimension but to Bautain and Günther exclusively. The answer is threefold.

The first reason for attending to Bautain and Günther alone is that they represent the farthest edges of the two sides of the debate, making their appropriation of the same epistemology the most intriguing. Second, the theologians associated with radical traditionalism did not appropriate the epistemology in question. Third, ontologism did not receive direct condemnation in *Dei*

---

21. A censure, in this case, means a reprimand.

22. The full list is as follows: *fideism* (Louis Bautain); *radical traditionalism* (Augustine Bonnetty); *rationalism* (James Frohschammer and Anton Günther); *ontologism* (Vincenzo Gioberti and Antonio Rosmini-Serbati) (John Paul II, *Fides et Ratio*, 69–70nn59–62, §52).

23. The other theologians are Georg Hermes, "the Tübingen theologians," including Johann Sebastian von Drey, and "the ontologists," including Vincenzo Gioberti and Antonio Rosmini-Serbati (McCool, *Nineteenth-Century Scholasticism*, 141). Elsewhere, McCool clarifies that Hermes "remained essentially Kantian in his philosophy," making him distinct from the rest of those who appropriated the epistemology of *Vernunft* (61).

INTRODUCTION

Filius. In sum, Bautain and Günther rest on and ideally represent a thread that runs from the lead-up to the council right into *Dei Filius* itself. Still, other theologians hold the potential for shining a light on new layers of *Dei Filius*. This book, it is hoped, encourages exploration of them.

Chapter 2 of this book is its briefest. The chapter begins with an overview of the condemnations of Bautain and Günther prior to the council. These condemnations anticipate the content and structure of *Dei Filius*. Next, a timeline of the council and of the composition of *Dei Filius* is provided. Chapter 3 of this book discusses key passages from each of the four chapters of *Dei Filius*. Key passages are those with a bearing on the relationship between faith and reason.

It was noted above that the nineteenth-century debate about the relationship between faith and reason *formally* ended with the promulgation of *Dei Filius*. Nevertheless, a new phenomenon, equally worthy of attention, sprang up: differing interpretations of *Dei Filius*. To neglect this would leave stones unturned and thus weaken the project of reassessment.

Among the extant interpretations of *Dei Filius*, this book attends to only one—that of Bernard Lonergan. As it happens, Lonergan's philosophical enterprise involves challenging the same epistemology that Kleutgen purportedly challenged in the lead-up to the First Vatican Council. Lonergan's interpretation of *Dei Filius* is found, first and foremost, in "Natural Knowledge of God," a paper presented at a convention in 1968.[24] Additionally, the teaching on natural knowledge of God in *Dei Filius* is referred to by Lonergan in 1957's *Insight* and 1972's *Method in Theology*. Chapter 4 of this book reviews this material chronologically. The chapter concludes with an evaluation of Lonergan's interpretation, which is consistent across the material.

The topic of natural knowledge of God is essential to an authentic reaction to the current growth of the view that faith and

24. Lonergan presented the paper at the twenty-third annual convention of the Catholic Theological Society of America, Washington, DC, June 17–20, 1968.

INTRODUCTION

reason are incompatible. There is another topic, however, that is little discussed today but equal in value as far as an authentic reaction is concerned. The topic is that of the role of reason in the lead-up to faith. It is referred to throughout this book more simply as acts that lead to faith. In *Dei Filius*, the mechanics of acts that lead to faith are thinly explicated, granting theologians significant—but not complete—freedom to develop an account. Lonergan does just this in "Analysis of Faith," a set of notes he prepared for students enrolled in a 1951–52 course. This set of notes captures the early Lonergan's stance on acts that lead to faith. A later stance can also be distinguished, marking a contrast with the essential consistency of his treatment of natural knowledge of God. That stance is found in *Method in Theology* and in the 1973 public lecture "Variations in Fundamental Theology." All of this material is reviewed in chapter 5. The chapter concludes with a critique of the mature—that is, the later—Lonergan's stance on acts that lead to faith.

To reiterate a crucial point once more, there exist other interpretations of *Dei Filius* and other accounts of acts that lead to faith that are worthy of exploration. Each that is explored contributes equally to the project of reassessment. This book, it is hoped, will inspire such work.

* * *

It is worth taking a moment to identify some topics that are relevant to this book's interests but will not be discussed in detail. The topics, which have received ample scholarly reflection elsewhere, are as follows: biblical characterizations of faith,[25] reason,[26] and the relationship between them;[27] portrayals of faith and reason by

---

25. R. W. L. Moberly, "אָמַן," *NIDOTTE* 1:427–33; R. Bultmann and A. Weiser, "*pisteúō*," in Kittel and Friedrich, *Theological Dictionary*, 849–57.

26. See "Scriptural Sources," ch. 2, in Haffner, *Mystery of Reason*.

27. See "Apologetics in the New Testament," ch. 1, in Dulles, *History of Apologetics*.

Introduction

noted theologians and philosophers;[28] and typologies of faith,[29] faith-reason relations,[30] and religion-science relations.[31]

---

28. See Dulles, *Assurance*, 204–8. For a selection of primary sources spanning from Plato to the present day, see Helm, *Faith and Reason*.
29. See Dulles, *Assurance*, 170–80.
30. See Basinger, "Faith/Reason Typologies."
31. See "Ways of Relating Science and Religion," ch. 4, in Barbour, *Religion and Science*. See also Barbour, "Relating Science and Religion."

1

McCool's Two Claims

IN THE NINETEENTH CENTURY, several Roman Catholic theologians received magisterial criticism for their views on faith and reason. The First Vatican Council's *Dei Filius* served as a final response to these theologians. Among them were Louis Eugène Marie Bautain (d. 1867) and Anton Günther (d. 1863). Bautain and Günther belonged to the opposed camps of fideism and rationalism. It comes as a surprise, then, to read the following claim by McCool: Bautain and Günther appropriated the same epistemology.[1] The epistemology in question revolves around a distinct view of the cognitive faculties of *Vernunft* (reason) and *Verstand* (understanding). McCool labels it "the post-Kantian epistemology of the intuitive *Vernunft*."[2] Henceforth it will be referred to simply as the epistemology of *Vernunft*.

McCool names Friedrich Heinrich Jacobi (d. 1819) as the principal representative of the epistemology of *Vernunft*.[3] The designation is an accurate one. As Arthur Lovejoy asserts, Jacobi was "the originator of [the] fashion of glorifying something

1. McCool, *Nineteenth-Century Scholasticism*, 141.
2. McCool, *Nineteenth-Century Scholasticism*, 143.
3. McCool, *Nineteenth-Century Scholasticism*, 141.

usually called 'the Reason' at the expense of 'the Understanding.'"[4] To be clear, it was the glorification and deprecation that were new in Jacobi; the faculties themselves had already been distinguished and elaborated on by Immanuel Kant (d. 1804). Later in this chapter, both Kant and Jacobi's views of *Vernunft* and *Verstand* will be attended to.

McCool states that it is Jacobi's version of the epistemology that influences Bautain.[5] With respect to Günther, McCool states that he was an adherent of the epistemology of *Vernunft* but does not invoke Jacobi's name. However, McCool does mention that Günther had a solid understanding of Friedrich Schelling (d. 1854)—another representative of the epistemology.[6] And Schelling, according to John Laughland, was "greatly influenced" by Jacobi.[7] In addition, McCool frequently refers to a text that at one point relays that Günther studied Jacobi.[8] Plainly, when one contemplates the epistemology of *Vernunft* and its influence on others, one ought to think primarily—but not exclusively—of Jacobi's epistemology. Later in this chapter, signs of the influence of the epistemology of *Vernunft* on Bautain and Günther will be traced.

McCool goes on to make a second surprising claim. He contends that prior to the First Vatican Council, neo-Thomists engaged in an "attack" on the epistemology of *Vernunft*.[9] The neo-Thomists believed that when this epistemology was embraced by a Roman Catholic theologian, it corrupted not only his or her view of philosophical method but of theological method, grace and nature, and faith and reason.[10] McCool names two persons in particular as carrying out this attack: Joseph Kleutgen (d. 1883) and

---

4. Lovejoy, *Reason, Understanding, and Time*, 4.

5. McCool, *Nineteenth-Century Scholasticism*, 48.

6. McCool, *Nineteenth-Century Scholasticism*, 88.

7. Laughland, *Schelling Versus Hegel*, 117. On the dispute between Jacobi and Schelling, see O'Meara, *Romantic Idealism and Catholicism*, 87.

8. The text is Schäfer, *Erkenntnistheoretische Kontroverse Kleutgen-Günther*, and the claim appears at 41n54.

9. McCool, *Nineteenth-Century Scholasticism*, 142.

10. McCool, *Nineteenth-Century Scholasticism*, 14.

Matteo Liberatore (d. 1892).[11] Kleutgen stands out as far as this chapter is concerned, for he would go on to be the main author of *Dei Filius*.[12] And as noted, *Dei Filius* served as a final response to the theologians who had been criticized for their views on the relationship between faith and reason, including Bautain and Günther.

McCool's two claims, when considered together, have the prospect of unveiling an additional layer of the articulation of the relationship between faith and reason in *Dei Filius*. It is indeed an unexpected prospect. One would not normally think that a dogmatic constitution of the Catholic Church on the topic of faith could be better understood through a consideration of its philosophical backdrop. What is more, a grasp of the philosophical backdrop of *Dei Filius* enhances the assessment of any thinker who has offered an interpretation of *Dei Filius*, as well as that figure's general perspective on the relationship between faith and reason. Chapters 4 and 5 of this book realize these points.

Given all the prospects above, it is worthwhile to further explore McCool's two claims. The second claim, regarding Kleutgen, will be explored first. As preparation for that task, it is prudent to sketch Kleutgen's background.

1.1 Assessing McCool's Second Claim

Joseph Wilhelm Karl Kleutgen was born in 1811 in Dortmund, a city in North Rhine-Westphalia, Germany. Among his early academic studies were philosophy courses at the University of Munich and the Academy at Münster.[13] John Inglis highlights that while in Münster, Kleutgen met church historian Johann Katerkamp (d. 1834) and likely learned from him an idea that would permeate his

---

11. McCool, *Nineteenth-Century Scholasticism*, 281n20.

12. McCool, *Nineteenth-Century Scholasticism*, 2. It should be registered, however, that Kleutgen was not involved in the preparation of the work of the council and was not in Rome at its opening (Granderath, *Concile du Vatican*, 2.2:12n4).

13. Inglis, *Spheres of Philosophical Inquiry*, 63, 67.

writings: the superiority of premodern philosophy and theology.¹⁴ In 1833 he attended seminary in Paderborn; the following year, he became a Jesuit novitiate in Brig, Switzerland.¹⁵ His philosophical and theological training took place in Fribourg. Interestingly, he learned of and had an admiration for Günther at this time.¹⁶ Ordained in 1837, he remained in Switzerland, teaching natural law and rhetoric.¹⁷ In 1843 he was sent to Rome. There he taught rhetoric at the German College and served as secretary to the General Superior of the Jesuits. In 1951 he became a consultor to the Congregation of the Index of Prohibited Books. As consultor, Kleutgen was ordered to examine the works of Günther; he was "instrumental" in the condemnation of them in 1857.¹⁸

Kleutgen authored two influential works in the mid-1800s: *Die Theologie der Vorzeit vertheidigt* (The theology of former times defended), published 1853–60, and *Die Philosophie der Vorzeit vertheidigt* (The philosophy of former times defended), published 1860–63.¹⁹ By former times, Kleutgen means premodern. The latter work is most important for the purposes of this chapter. In it, as John Inglis states, "Kleutgen claims that a common theory [of knowledge] . . . was current among a number of significant pre-modern theologians, including Augustine, Anselm, Aquinas, Suarez, and Silvester Maurus."²⁰ For Kleutgen, this common

---

14. Inglis, *Spheres of Philosophical Inquiry*, 67–68. Inglis bases this assessment on Deufel, *Kirche und Tradition*, 35.

15. Inglis, *Spheres of Philosophical Inquiry*, 69.

16. Vincelette, *Recent Catholic Philosophy: The Nineteenth Century*, 123. This work will be referred to hereafter as *Recent Catholic Philosophy*, but note that it is distinct from Vincelette's follow-up, *Recent Catholic Philosophy: The Twentieth Century*.

17. Vincelette, *Recent Catholic Philosophy*, 122–23.

18. Inglis, *Spheres of Philosophical Inquiry*, 78, 80.

19. On the addition of volumes and other changes in subsequent editions, see McCool, *Nineteenth-Century Scholasticism*, 174–75. Note that McCool seems to imply (incorrectly) that the second edition of *Die Philosophie der Vorzeit vertheidigt* was a single volume. For the changes in list form, see Lakner, "Kleutgen," 209–214.

20. Inglis, *Spheres of Philosophical Inquiry*, 91.

McCool's Two Claims

theory of knowledge "can serve as a basis for contemporary epistemological concerns."[21] Drawing from this common theory, Kleutgen addresses the relationship between faith and reason; he argues for a middle path between rationalism and fideism (the then-contemporary forms).[22] Peter Walter holds that *Die Philosophie der Vorzeit vertheidigt* "may be regarded as the most important philosophical work of the incipient neo-scholasticism in Germany."[23]

Kleutgen's most notable role came in 1870 when he was asked to help with the composition of *Dei Filius*. Chapter 2 of this book will detail Kleutgen's role in composing the document. Notably, *Dei Filius* is not the only magisterial document treating faith and reason that Kleutgen had a hand in. He is rumored to have composed the first draft of the 1879 encyclical *Aeterni Patris*.[24] Kleutgen ultimately returned to teaching, including as professor of dogmatic theology at the Gregorian University. He passed away in 1883.[25]

McCool's claim that Kleutgen engaged in an attack on the epistemology of *Vernunft* can now be assessed. The need for assessment arises chiefly from the fact that McCool does not provide primary source references for the claim. Fortunately, McCool dates the attack to the time of the publication of *Die Philosophie der Vorzeit vertheidigt*.[26] Now, the edition of the work that will be used in what follows was published in 1878; it is the second edition, and it contains revisions. The reader is right to be concerned that this edition may feature views that Kleutgen did not hold when *Dei Filius* was promulgated on April 24, 1870. The simple remedy to this, namely, utilizing the first edition, is not possible due

---

21. Inglis, *Spheres of Philosophical Inquiry*, 91.

22. Vincelette, *Recent Catholic Philosophy*, 125.

23. Walter, "Neuscholastische Philosophie," 2:145. Here and beyond, translations are personal unless otherwise noted.

24. McCool, *Nineteenth-Century Scholasticism*, 2.

25. Vincelette, *Recent Catholic Philosophy*, 124. On Kleutgen's misdeeds, see Wolf, *Nuns of Sant'Ambrogio*, 271–319.

26. McCool, *Nineteenth-Century Scholasticism*, 137–38.

to its inaccessibility. What is accessible is the authorized French translation of the work, published between 1868 and 1870.[27] The first three volumes of this translation were published before the promulgation of *Dei Filius*. Moreover, Kleutgen signed off on the fourth volume before—or at least, very close to—the promulgation as well, given its imprimatur date of June 4, 1870. In what follows, every reference is to the 1878 edition but confirmed to also appear in the French translation without significant change. Any instances of significant change will be registered within footnotes.

Assessing McCool's second claim is made easier by the fact that only a few pages into the introduction of *Die Philosophie der Vorzeit vertheidigt*, Kleutgen makes reference to "Jacobi's school."[28] What is more, he immediately discusses Jacobi's glorification of *Vernunft* at the expense of *Verstand*. Such is one of numerous references to Jacobi in the work.

An assessment must also attend to a part of the work entitled "On the Difference Between Reason and Understanding." There Kleutgen compares *Vernunft* and *Verstand* with what he contends are their Scholastic alternatives: *intellectus* (understanding) and *ratio* (reason).[29] The pairing is based on a distinction regularly employed medieval thinkers. As Joseph Koterski explains,

> Often *ratio* is used to refer specifically to thinking through an issue discursively (that is, in step-by-step fashion), and in this usage it stands in contrast to *intellectus*, which is the term that tends to be used in the sense of intellectual insight or intuition, that is, the grasp of some point without any apparent mental process.[30]

27. Kleutgen, *Philosophie scolastique*.
28. Kleutgen, *Philosophie der Vorzeit*, 1:8, §6.
29. Kleutgen, *Philosophie der Vorzeit*, 1:234, §145.
30. Koterski, *Introduction to Medieval Philosophy*, 11. Aquinas writes, "Intelligence and reason are not different powers, yet they are named after different acts. For intelligence takes its name from being an intimate penetration of the truth, while reason is so called from being inquisitive and discursive" (Aquinas, *Summa Theologica*, 2:1404, II-II, q. 49, a. 5, ad. 3). The basis for Aquinas's distinction dates to the classical period. In commentaries on Aristotle's works, "*nous* (not *dianoia* or *ratio*) is the evident source of Aquinas's *intellectus*" (Tallon, *Head and Heart*, 277).

McCool's Two Claims

Kleutgen's pairing of *Vernunft* with *intellectus* and *Verstand* with *ratio* shows—for reasons to be discussed shortly—that his concern in this section is with Jacobi and other representatives of the epistemology of *Vernunft*. This is not to say that Kant is not a concern for Kleutgen here or elsewhere in *Die Philosophie der Vorzeit vertheidigt*; there are many references to him. What one notices about those references, however, is that they are mostly in passing.[31] Kant is a culprit in the extra-church perception of weakness in the philosophy of former times—that is clear. What concerns Kleutgen more is that which has caused an intra-church perception of weakness in the philosophy of former times.

Another element of McCool's second claim is that neo-Thomists, such as Kleutgen, judged that a Catholic thinker who embraces the epistemology of *Vernunft* necessarily corrupts not only his or her view of philosophical method but also of theological method, grace and nature, and faith and reason. As before, McCool does not supply primary source references for this claim. It is fortunate that early in the introduction of *Die Philosophie der Vorzeit vertheidigt*, Kleutgen states that Bautain, Günther, and others sought out a new approach in their effort to fight modern unbelief—an approach that involved concessions to the movement they were fighting against. As to what the new approach entails, Kleutgen states that they sought "a new basis of all knowledge."[32] There is no mention, however, of *Vernunft* or Jacobi. Kleutgen goes on to speak of the "school that arose in France," which is a clear reference to Bautain, but once again, neither *Vernunft* nor Jacobi is invoked.[33] Later in the work, Kleutgen states that people have "vainly" searched for Jacobi's view of *Vernunft* in the writings of Clement (d. ca. 215), Origen (d. ca. 253), and Augustine of Hippo (d. 430).[34] As will be discussed shortly, Bautain is one of the people

---

31. The exception is *Philosophie der Vorzeit*, 1:563–86, §§354–68, where Kleutgen tackles Kant's theory of space and time.

32. Kleutgen, *Philosophie der Vorzeit*, 1:12, §9.

33. Kleutgen, *Philosophie der Vorzeit*, 1:17, §13.

34. Kleutgen, *Philosophie der Vorzeit*, 1:756, §471. This is an instance where the French translation slightly differs. In it, Kleutgen meagerly states that

who did just this; even though Kleutgen does not invoke Bautain's name, it is likely that he has him in mind. Overall, there is only a hint of corruption via the epistemology of *Vernunft* regarding Bautain. There is far less ambiguity when it comes to Günther.

Kleutgen explicitly ties Günther to the epistemology of *Vernunft*.[35] And there are three passages, with a descending degree of directness, in which Kleutgen deems the corruption of Günther's philosophical method, theological method, and so on, a result of appropriating the epistemology of *Vernunft*. First, he contends that Jacobi and Günther use the term "faith" in a similar way within their theories of knowledge.[36] Second, he reports that according to Günther, Scholasticism cannot adequately maintain the distinction between spirit and nature or God and world, nor can it determine the correct relation between knowledge and faith.[37] And it is implied that Günther's adoption of a new approach to establish integrity in these three areas led to the corruption of them. Finally, Kleutgen contends that Günther "distorted" the Holy Trinity in order to "defend a philosophical error."[38] The error in question falls under the umbrella of epistemology, although *Vernunft* itself is not referred to.

The reader might ask at this juncture who the "other" theologians were that Kleutgen contends sought out a new approach in their effort to fight modern unbelief. The question is a fair one since any other Catholic thinker deemed to appropriate the epistemology of *Vernunft* and, as a result, corrupt his or her theological method, and so on, would corroborate McCool's second claim. The other theologians named by Kleutgen are Félicité de Lamennais (d. 1854), Vincenzo Gioberti (d. 1852), and

---

one cannot support Jacobi's view of *Vernunft* using the writings of Clement, Origen, and Augustine.

35. Kleutgen, *Philosophie der Vorzeit*, 1:156, §96. While it is too early to unpack, the nuance of McCool's full label "the post-Kantian epistemology of the intuitive *Vernunft*" should be noticed, for Kleutgen claims that Günther did not make a case for "intellectual intuition" (1:18, §13).

36. Kleutgen, *Philosophie der Vorzeit*, 1:399, §260.

37. Kleutgen, *Philosophie der Vorzeit*, 1:20, 135, §§15, 83.

38. Kleutgen, *Philosophie der Vorzeit*, 1:211, §129.

Georg Hermes (d. 1831).[39] Lamennais can be ruled out quickly, for Kleutgen explicitly separates him from the way Jacobi uses the term "faith."[40] With respect to Gioberti, the epistemology of *Vernunft* is not mentioned amid the small number of references to him. The last thinker in the list, Hermes, cannot be so quickly passed over.

Kleutgen does indeed state that Hermes deprecates the philosophy of former times for not distinguishing *Vernunft* and *Verstand* in human thinking[41]—a failure that meant the Scholastic doctrines of God and creation contained mistakes.[42] At the same time, Kleutgen contends that Hermes "strongly opposes" Jacobi's epistemology,[43] and he states that Hermes's standpoint and method differs from that of Günther.[44] Hermes is something of a unique figure, then, within the philosophical backdrop of *Dei Filius*. He is significant, to be sure, but he receives half as many references as Günther in *Die Philosophie der Vorzeit vertheidigt*. One can make better sense of this when one learns that Günther "went beyond Hermes," as Alan Vincelette puts it. While it is jumping ahead to state it, the way in which he went beyond Hermes was in declaring that the "individual contents [of revelation] could be proven through reason."[45] Here lies the basis for investigating Bautain and Günther rather than Bautain and Hermes in this book; that the former pair (purportedly) appropriated the same epistemology is more surprising than the latter pair and thus has greater potential for understanding the unique philosophical backdrop of *Dei Filius*.[46] Still, Hermes stands as a figure whose treatment by Kleutgen further corroborates McCool's second claim.

39. Kleutgen, *Philosophie der Vorzeit*, 1:12, §9.
40. Kleutgen, *Philosophie der Vorzeit*, 1:399, §260.
41. Kleutgen, *Philosophie der Vorzeit*, 1:134, §82.
42. Kleutgen, *Philosophie der Vorzeit*, 1:19, §14.
43. Kleutgen, *Philosophie der Vorzeit*, 1:130–31, §§80–81.
44. Kleutgen, *Philosophie der Vorzeit*, 1:135, §83.
45. Vincelette, *Recent Catholic Philosophy*, 56. See also Reardon, *Religion in Romanticism*, 126.
46. The complete rationale for not exploring additional theologians is

Reassessing Faith and Reason

1.2 Assessing McCool's First Claim

To reiterate, McCool's first claim is that Bautain and Günther, despite belonging to the opposed camps of fideism and rationalism, both appropriated the epistemology of *Vernunft*. Plainly, an accurate assessment of this claim requires an account of the epistemology of *Vernunft* that is not influenced by McCool's—or Kleutgen's, for that matter—characterization of it. Such an account would seem to be achieved simply by outlining Jacobi's epistemology, with an emphasis on its treatment of *Vernunft* and *Verstand*. However, it was Kant's epistemology, and his own treatment of the two faculties, that provoked Jacobi to put forth his view. It is therefore prudent to outline Kant's view first.

It should be stressed that the outlines that follow relay only what is necessary to understand and assess McCool's second claim; they are not exhaustive. As part of this approach, only the major works of the two philosophers will be appealed to. The outline of Kant will draw exclusively from the *Critique of Pure Reason*, which was first published in 1781, with a second edition in 1787.[47] The outline of Jacobi will draw exclusively from *David Hume on Faith, or Idealism and Realism*, first published in 1787 (subsequent to the publication of the second edition of the *Critique*), followed by a second edition in 1815.[48]

Kant

Let us focus on three of the cognitive faculties that Kant delineates in the *Critique of Pure Reason*: *Sinnlichkeit* (sensibility), *Verstand* (understanding), and *Vernunft* (reason).[49] The faculty of *Verstand* produces concepts. In order for concepts not to be "empty," *Verstand* must draw upon the faculty of *Sinnlichkeit*.[50] *Sinnlichkeit*

---

provided in this book's introduction.
47. German: *Kritik der reinen Vernunft*.
48. Jacobi, *Main Philosophical Writings*; *Werke*.
49. Kant, *Critique of Pure Reason*, 250, B283.
50. Kant, *Critique of Pure Reason*, 93, B75.

produces "sensible intuitions."⁵¹ *Sinnlichkeit* is constituted in such a way that every sensible intuition is framed in "space and time, the . . . forms of sensibility."⁵² This spatiotemporal framing has a momentous epistemic implication. In the first edition, Kant writes, "[A] [kind of] knowledge must be possible, in which there is no sensibility, and which alone has reality that is absolutely objective."⁵³ Returning to the second edition, Kant denies precisely this kind of knowledge to human beings. He writes, "We cannot in the least represent to ourselves the possibility of an understanding which should know its object, not discursively through categories, but intuitively in a non-sensible intuition."⁵⁴ Only in the mind of the primordial being is an *intellektuelle Anschauung* (intellectual intuition) possible.⁵⁵ Consequently, the human mind does not grasp "things in themselves," but rather "appearances, that is, mere representations."⁵⁶ Even though things in themselves are genuinely real and somehow responsible for one's sensible intuitions, they elude human knowing.

There remains the faculty of *Vernunft*. Kant contends that *Vernunft* has a descending function and an ascending function.⁵⁷ The descending function is to link together the individual judgments that the understanding yields by way of syllogistic inferences. The ascending function is to demand "the unconditioned," that is, "the *totality* of the *conditions* for any given conditioned."⁵⁸ This demand

51. Kant, *Critique of Pure Reason*, 105, B93.
52. Kant, *Critique of Pure Reason*, 175, B169.
53. Kant, *Critique of Pure Reason*, 267, A250.
54. Kant, *Critique of Pure Reason*, 272–73, B311–12.
55. Kant, *Critique of Pure Reason*, 90, B72. As Moltke Gram observes, "Kant indiscriminately uses one term to include three different kinds of intellectual intuition" ("Intellectual Intuition," 304). The first kind, according to Gram, entails "an intellect that knows things in themselves independently of any conditions of sensibility" (288). In this chapter, the first kind is taken to exemplify Kant's position.
56. Kant, *Critique of Pure Reason*, 439, B518–19.
57. Kant, *Critique of Pure Reason*, 321, B388. For a fuller explanation of the two functions, see Gardner, *Kant and the "Critique,"* 216–17.
58. Kant, *Critique of Pure Reason*, 316, B379; emphasis in original. For

stems from the fact that the major premise of one syllogism is often dependent upon the conclusion of some other syllogism, thus *Vernunft* aspires to find that which has no conditions whatsoever: the totality of conditions.[59]

Kant states that because there are three forms of syllogisms—categorical, hypothetical, and disjunctive—there arise in the course of *Vernunft*'s demand for the unconditioned three corresponding ideas: the soul, the world, and God.[60] If these ideas could be verified in experience, then one could justifiably deem *Vernunft* a majestic faculty, but they cannot: "We can never transcend the limits of possible experience."[61] As a result, the ideas of *Vernunft* "never allow of any constitutive employment" but only a "regulative employment, namely, that of directing the understanding towards a certain goal."[62] Kant maintains that the idea of God and the idea of an afterlife issue from "reason in its practical employment."[63] Consequently, "no one . . . will be able to boast that he *knows* that there is a God, and a future life"; one can have only "*moral* certainty."[64]

---

analysis of Kant's notion of the unconditioned and a survey of his contemporaries' reactions to it, see Ameriks, *Kant and Historical Turn*, 149–60.

59. Kant, *Critique of Pure Reason*, 306, B364.

60. Kant, *Critique of Pure Reason*, 322–24, B390–92. For analysis, see Grier, *Kant's Doctrine of Transcendental Illusion*, 130–39.

61. Kant, *Critique of Pure Reason*, 24, Bxix. As Paul Guyer observes, "Ideas of the unconditioned are fundamentally incompatible with the structure of our sensible intuition, which is always conditioned—remember, every region of space can only be represented as part of a larger space, and every region of time only as part of a larger time. In other words, it is the most fundamental characteristic of our intuitions that they are always conditioned by further intuitions, and so nothing unconditioned can ever be 'given' or represented in our sensible intuition; no representation of space or time is ever complete. Therefore nothing unconditioned can ever be an object of knowledge for us" (*Kant*, 133).

62. Kant, *Critique of Pure Reason*, 533, B672. For analysis, see Guyer, *Kant*, 166–67.

63. Kant, *Critique of Pure Reason*, 634, B831.

64. Kant, *Critique of Pure Reason*, 650, B856–57; emphasis in original.

Jacobi

Jacobi's novel understanding of *Vernunft* and *Verstand* emerges in a mature form only in his later writings, but it is within his early writings that he identifies what will eventually provoke his novel understanding. In the supplement to the 1787 edition of *David Hume on Faith, or Idealism and Realism*, Jacobi interprets Kant's notion of things in themselves as an attempt to avoid the logically consistent implication of his philosophy. Jacobi describes the implication this way:

> What we realists call actual objects or things independent of our representations are for the transcendental idealist only internal beings which exhibit nothing at all of a thing that may perhaps be there outside us, or to which the appearance may refer. Rather, these internal beings are merely subjective determinations of the mind, entirely void of anything truly objective.[65]

In response to Kant, Jacobi contends that human beings possess an immediate certainty about the actuality—that is, the extra-mental existence—of both sensible and supersensible things. The early Jacobi invokes the terms *Gefühl* (feeling) and *Glaube* (faith/belief) in defending his view. Although he is not consistent, he usually refers to feeling as the faculty involved and faith or belief as one's assurance of the actuality of things.[66] As Samuel Atlas explains,

> Objects have to be given to us through immediate feeling or faith before thought comes into play. The task of discursive thinking is to observe, analyze, compare, and order perceptions by reducing them to their fundamental principles. But unless something real is previously given through feeling, discursive thinking cannot take place.[67]

---

65. Jacobi, *Main Philosophical Writings*, 334. Italics have been removed here and in ensuing quotations. For an evaluation of Jacobi's interpretation of Kant on this matter, see Gram, "Things in Themselves."

66. Crawford, *Philosophy of F. H. Jacobi*, 34.

67. Atlas, "Jacobi, Friedrich Heinrich," 4:769.

Reassessing Faith and Reason

The employment of the term "faith" has a clear religious connotation that Jacobi upholds in other discussions about one's assurance of the actuality of things. For example, when contemplating a term to describe "the means through which [man] partakes of the certainty of external objects *qua* things existing independently of his representation of them," Jacobi asks, "[Is there] a more apt word than 'revelation'?"[68]

Turning to the later Jacobi, it is plain that he is still driven by concerns about the true implication of the *Critique of Pure Reason*. In the preface to the 1815 edition of *David Hume on Faith*, Jacobi states that Kantian philosophy "pretends to be a non-idealism"[69] but in fact "leads necessarily to a system of absolute subjectivity."[70] In response, Jacobi contends that human beings can acquire knowledge of sensible things through a *sinnliche Anschauung* (sense intuition) and of supersensible things through a *rationale Anschauung* (rational intuition).[71] Jacobi correlates the former kind of intuition with the faculty of *Sinnlichkeit*[72] and the latter kind with the faculty of *Vernunft*.[73]

Although "knowledge of God"[74] is obtainable through a *rationale Anschauung*, its use would seem to be extremely restricted, given that *Verstand* is, as Crawford relays, "the only faculty of explanation or interpretation." Jacobi "tried to ... limit himself to little more than bare affirmations of content." Crawford continues, "But he did not remain true to his self-made limitations," particularly in his later writings.[75]

---

68. Jacobi, *Main Philosophical Writings*, 272.
69. Jacobi, *Main Philosophical Writings*, 554.
70. Jacobi, *Main Philosophical Writings*, 552.
71. Jacobi: *Main Philosophical Writings*, 563; *Werke*, 2:59–60.
72. Jacobi, *Main Philosophical Writings*, 562.
73. Jacobi, *Main Philosophical Writings*, 563.
74. Jacobi, *Main Philosophical Writings*, 564.
75. Crawford, *Philosophy of F. H. Jacobi*, 45.

Bautain

With Kant and Jacobi in view, an assessment of McCool's claim that Bautain appropriated the epistemology of *Vernunft* is now possible. As with Kleutgen, it is prudent to take a moment to provide a brief biography of Bautain.

Bautain was born in Paris in 1796.[76] He attended the École Normale, studying under philosopher Victor Cousin (d. 1867). According to Bernard Reardon, the "strong admixture of Platonism" in Cousin's teaching had a "lasting effect" on Bautain.[77] Bautain earned a Doctor of Letters with the title of Philosophy Scholar in 1816.[78] The same year he was appointed chair of philosophy first at the Collège Royal of Strasbourg, then at the University of Strasbourg.[79] During this time, Bautain lost his faith.

According to Paul Poupard, Bautain was "attracted by Jacobi's thought," enough so that he travelled to meet Jacobi in person in 1818.[80] Recalling the meeting in a letter written the following year, Bautain remarks, "I was never able to get into his theories, I was never able to take something firm and systematic from him."[81] During the same trip, Bautain met Schelling, another representative of the epistemology of *Vernunft*. Thinking back to that meeting, Bautain writes, "I did not understand all of his doctrine, but I think I understood the spirit of it."[82] These two meetings do not clearly signal an appropriation of the epistemology. In the years that followed, however, evidence of Jacobi's influence is stronger. For example, Bautain's return to the Catholic faith in 1820 was due in part to Louise Humann's (d. 1836) recommendation that he read three authors: Jacobi, Kant, and Franz von Baader (d. 1841).

---

76. This biography draws extensively from Vincelette, *Recent Catholic Philosophy*, 34–35. Sources other than Vincelette will be noted.
77. Reardon, *Liberalism and Tradition*, 117.
78. Régny, *Abbé Bautain*, 9–10.
79. Régny, *Abbé Bautain*, 10.
80. Poupard, *Essai de philosophie chrétienne*, 71n2.
81. Poupard, *Essai de philosophie chrétienne*, 71n2.
82. Poupard, *Essai de philosophie chrétienne*, 74.

Baader, it is worth noting, "[saw] no other means of getting out of Kant's subjectivism than the path taken by . . . Jacobi," according to Franz Lakner.[83] Whatever other exposure Bautain gained to Jacobi's epistemology in the ensuing years, it sufficed to yield a strong contrast with the letter of 1819. Bautain's mature philosophy is, in the judgment of Josef Geiselmann, "undoubtedly inspired by Jacobi."[84]

When Bautain returned to Catholicism, it was as a proponent of fideism. This led to his suspension from teaching in 1822. At this point, he pursued doctorates in medicine and theology at the University of Strasbourg and, in 1828, became a diocesan priest. He was then appointed director of the minor seminary in Strasbourg, but here too, because of his promotion of fideism, he was suspended in 1834. This ordeal, which reached its peak with Pope Gregory XVI asking Bautain to sign propositions against fideism in 1840, will be taken up at the beginning of chapter 2.

Although Bautain began publishing when he earned his Doctor of Letters, his writing did not catch on in the public until 1833.[85] In 1835 Bautain published his most well-known work, *La philosophie du christianisme: Correspondance religieuse de L. Bautain* (The philosophy of Christianity: Religious correspondence by L. Bautain). As Vincelette explains, this two-volume work "represents an exchange of philosophical letters between Bautain (Le Maître) and his pupils."[86] Beyond this, Bautain published many books,[87] including *Philosophie: Psychologie expérimentale* (Philosophy: Experimental psychology) in 1839.

Bautain travelled to Rome to try to repair his reputation. As Vincelette reports, he met the Thomist Giovanni Perrone (d. 1876), began to study Aquinas, and ultimately "became convinced

---

83. Lakner, "Kleutgen," 170.

84. Geiselmann, *Meaning of Tradition*, 65. Similarly, Avery Dulles states that Bautain was "influenced by the intuitionism of Jacobi" (Dulles, *Assurance*, 82).

85. Reardon, *Liberalism and Tradition*, 119.

86. Vincelette, *Recent Catholic Philosophy*, 35.

87. For a complete list, see Régny, *Abbé Bautain*, 476–79.

of errors in his earlier views."[88] As a result, his position as director of the minor seminary was restored. Later, he served as dean of the Faculty of Letters at the University of Strasbourg, vicar general for the archdiocese of Paris, and professor of moral theology at the Sorbonne. Bautain died in Viroflay on October 15, 1867.

McCool provides only secondary sources to support his claim that Bautain appropriated the epistemology of *Vernunft*. This is understandable for two reasons: first, the apparent absence of a direct admission of such appropriation, and second, the necessity of reliance on scholars who have endured the task of extracting Bautain's philosophy from the several stylistically varied writings that contain it. The assessment that follows, too, regularly makes use of secondary sources.

In *Philosophie: Psychologie expérimentale*, Bautain states that *l'intelligence* (intelligence) and *la raison* (reason) are "distinct faculties of the human mind."[89] What is important for the purposes of this chapter is Bautain's discussion of these two faculties in relation to Kant. What he says must be attended to closely, for the terminology employed can generate confusion when Kant's German and Bautain's French are translated into English. Bautain states that Kant associated the power of conceiving ideas with *Vernunft* but should have associated this power with what Bautain calls intelligence.[90] It is reason, for Bautain, that produces concepts. Now, this is only a small source of the confusion in question. The main source lies in Bautain's valuation of the two faculties. Walter Marshall Horton provides a clear summation:

> [Bautain] insists upon [reason's] incurable tendency to reduce concrete and organic reality to a series of disconnected abstractions. Kant's judgment of it was quite correct; it is a purely phenomenal and subjective faculty,

88. Vincelette, *Recent Catholic Philosophy*, 35. Interestingly, one of Perrone's disciples was Johannes Baptist Franzelin (d. 1886), who would go on to compose an early schema of *Dei Filius*.

89. Bautain, *Philosophie: Psychologie expérimentale*, 2:359. Attention is drawn to this and some other references in this section by the authors of various secondary sources appealed to.

90. Bautain, *Philosophie: Psychologie expérimentale*, 1:200.

and its views of reality are simply convenient points of view.... [If] we can escape from the phenomenal world, it is only by virtue of a superior faculty, the intelligence, which seizes at a glance the genetic order and nature of things.[91]

The depiction of the faculty of *reason* as the inferior faculty conflicts with the English-language habit that Lovejoy was seen to adopt at the outset of this chapter. Once one breaks this habit, one can properly search for signs of an appropriation of the epistemology of *Vernunft* in Bautain.

As Poupard relays, Bautain praises Plato's firm distinction between *nous* and *dianoia*—a distinction that parallels, but is not identical to, Bautain's distinction between intelligence and reason.[92] One can see this on display when Bautain speaks of "intellectual vision or the gaze of the intelligence" wherein there is "no active reflection, no mixture of thought."[93] For Bautain, "apprehending the truth instantly" is the hallmark of intelligence; reason is "always complex, successive, fractional."[94] These statements clearly echo Plato, but he is not the sole inspiration for Bautain's distinction.

Already hinted at by Horton in the passage above, Bautain was also inspired—or better, impacted—by Kant. As Vincelette states, Bautain accepts Kant's view that human beings cannot acquire knowledge of things in themselves or the existence of God through discursive or syllogistic means.[95] Bautain breaks with Kant, however, by asserting that human beings *can* acquire knowledge of the nature of things and the existence of God by means of the faculty of intelligence. How such knowledge is acquired must

---

91. Horton, *Philosophy of Abbé Bautain*, 189. See Bautain, *Philosophie: Psychologie expérimentale*, 2:364.

92. Poupard, *Essai de philosophie chrétienne*, 259.

93. Bautain, *Philosophie: Psychologie expérimentale*, 2:372.

94. Bautain, *Philosophie: Psychologie expérimentale*, 2:364.

95. Vincelette, *Recent Catholic Philosophy*, 36. See Bautain, *Philosophie du christianisme*, 1:173. See also, in translation, Bautain, "Letter on God's Existence," 158.

be approached cautiously, as Bautain is not entirely consistent with his terminology in this area.

Horton explains that for Bautain, there is an "Eternal Light whose beams are incessantly beating upon us in the endeavor to communicate the Truth to us."[96] Bautain sees "sudden illuminations, visions, auditions, [and] ecstasies" as "direct communication between the soul or intelligence and supersensible reality."[97] The nuance of soul *or* intelligence made by Horton is important. On the one hand, Bautain speaks of "men of genius" who grasped universal truths through "intellectual intuition,"[98] and on the other, he speaks of "prophets" and "apostles" who grasped universal truths through an intellectual intuition, as well as an intuition of the soul.[99]

Those in the two categories above are not the only recipients of divine communication. Bautain gives an example of a third category: you are listening to a person speaking when, suddenly, "without reflection, . . . the ray of the Truth reaches you," and "the seed of a new idea is fertilized in your understanding."[100] Since human beings have been created with a hunger for ultimate reality, and since "ideas are correlative to eternal ideals," as Horton puts it, upon exposure to an idea from another mind there is an immediate "taste" for its truth.[101] Importantly, the pool of ideas tied to all three groups constitutes tradition, and tradition dates back to the moment when God shared an idea with Adam in the garden of Eden, stirring his mind into action.[102] This event, known as primitive revelation, was integrated into Bautain's and many others' philosophies.

---

96. Horton, *Philosophy of Abbé Bautain*, 151.
97. Horton, *Philosophy of Abbé Bautain*, 178.
98. Bautain, *Philosophie: Psychologie expérimentale*, 1:102.
99. Horton, *Philosophy of Abbé Bautain*, 183.
100. Bautain, *Philosophie: Psychologie expérimentale*, 2:25.
101. Horton, *Philosophy of Abbé Bautain*, 226–27. Bautain is seen here taking a stance on a long-standing discussion regarding divine ideas and truth. See Lisska, *Aquinas's Theory of Perception*, 87.
102. Horton, *Philosophy of Abbé Bautain*, 185.

Reassessing Faith and Reason

The remaining aspect of Bautain's philosophy in need of inspection is his view of faith. "Faith," writes Bautain, "is an intelligence penetrated by the action of truth."[103] This characterization of faith "must have come" from Jacobi, according to Horton.[104] Now, as Poupard notes, and many others agree, "the great vulnerability of Bautain's system stems from the ambivalence of his notion of faith."[105] With this in mind, his notion can be considered. Bautain describes the unfolding of faith within the faculty of intelligence as follows:

> The intelligence participates, through faith in the word of God, in the supernatural light contained therein; at first it receives it without understanding it, but soon, if man persists, his intelligence is enlightened as his heart is touched, and he understands what he had at first believed.[106]

The epistemic fruit of such participation is insisted on by Bautain. As Reardon sums it up, "Faith . . . leads to self-evidence, knowledge, absolute certitude."[107] Even though "the independent demands of the intelligence must . . . be met,"[108] which ensures that faith is not blind, the upshot of the position places Bautain under the umbrella of fideism. He rejects arguments for the existence of God, as well as arguments for the credibility of revelation that are based on miracles and prophecies.[109]

103. Bautain, *Philosophie: Psychologie expérimentale*, 2:376.
104. Horton, *Philosophy of Abbé Bautain*, 71.
105. Poupard, *Essai de philosophie chrétienne*, 370.
106. Bautain, *Résumé des conférences*, 11, §13; quoted in Poupard, *Essai de philosophie chrétienne*, 328. Note that this statement was made after Bautain signed propositions against fideism in 1840. For the later Bautain's views, see Horton, *Philosophy of Abbé Bautain*, 208, 288.
107. Reardon, *Liberalism and Tradition*, 132.
108. Reardon, *Liberalism and Tradition*, 127n45.
109. Horton explains: "He puts prophecy, miracle, and historical testimony in quite a secondary place, denying the possibility of basing a case on such evidence; and he appeals directly to the faith-awakening power of the Book which contains the revelation, and the Church which announces it—a power due to the perfect correspondence between the Gospel and the soul's need"

Günther

Günther was born in Lindenau, Bohemia, in 1783.[110] He studied law and philosophy at the University of Prague, beginning in 1803. McCool reports that among the philosophers he gained exposure to at this time were Kant and Schelling.[111] He also studied Jacobi at some point, according to Theo Schäfer.[112] In 1811 he abandoned the field of law and began to study theology, a decision which ultimately led to being ordained a diocesan priest in 1820.[113] Günther then entered the Jesuit novitiate; however, as McCool relays, "he and his Jesuit superiors came to an amicable agreement that his vocation was to work alone."[114] He settled in Vienna in 1824, working as a scholar, tutor, and government censor of books.

Günther published a great number of works, amongst which were the two-volume *Vorschule zur spekulativen Theologie des positiven Christenthums* (Propaedeutic to the speculative theology of positive Christianity) in 1828 and 1829, and, with Johann Heinrich Pabst (d. 1838), *Janusköpfe für Philosophie und Theologie* (Janus heads for philosophy and theology) in 1834.[115] Underlying his works are the goals of "bringing Christian apologetics up to date" and "making theology sufficiently scientific to impress even unbelievers," as Reardon explains.[116] His works won him "acclaim among German-speaking Catholic intellectuals."[117] However, his use of philosophical dialogue, which as McCool states was already

---

(*Philosophy of Abbé Bautain*, 228). See also Reardon, *Liberalism and Tradition*, 135.

110. This biography draws extensively from Vincelette, *Recent Catholic Philosophy*, 55–56. Sources other than Vincelette will be noted.

111. McCool, *Nineteenth-Century Scholasticism*, 88.

112. Schäfer, *Erkenntnistheoretische kontroverse Kleutgen-Günther*, 41n54.

113. Reardon, *Religion in Romanticism*, 126.

114. McCool, *Nineteenth-Century Scholasticism*, 89.

115. For a complete list, see Pritz, *Glauben und Wissen*, 7–8.

116. Reardon, *Religion in Romanticism*, 127.

117. Reardon, *Religion in Romanticism*, 126–27.

an "outmoded" style in Günther's time, led to a neglect of his works in the decades that followed.[118]

Neglect of Günther's works was exacerbated by their placement on the Index of Prohibited Books in 1857. Although he "accepted" the prohibition, reports Reardon, he did so "unwillingly and with some bitterness of heart."[119] This and other magisterial criticisms of Günther will be discussed in more detail at the beginning of chapter 2.

With such immense scholarly output, the question arises as to whether Günther ever served as an instructor at a university. As Reardon explains, "Over the years, he received a number of invitations to take up professorships at universities in Germany." Reardon continues, "[He] declined them all, hoping perhaps for the offer of such a post at Vienna, though this never came his way."[120] Günther passed away in Vienna in 1863.

Almost all of the references that McCool provides to support his claim that Günther appropriated the epistemology of *Vernunft* are either reproductions of his writings within secondary sources or secondary sources themselves. As it was with Bautain, one cannot help but rely on scholars who have laboured to extract Günther's philosophy from the multitude of stylistically varied writings that contain it. In a collection of excerpts from the writings of Catholics in the nineteenth century, Günther's text is deemed "the most difficult one in the volume."[121] Once more, then, the outline that follows frequently makes use of secondary sources.

Günther is animated by a desire to update apologetics, as already noted, but also, as Reardon states, to challenge "the pantheistic tendencies of contemporary idealist philosophy, in particular, Hegelianism."[122] Günther's commitments in the latter endeavour carry over into his strategy for the former. Vincelette relays that Günther judged the cause of Georg Hegel's (d. 1831) pantheism

118. McCool, *Nineteenth-Century Scholasticism*, 90.
119. Reardon, *Religion in Romanticism*, 126.
120. Reardon, *Religion in Romanticism*, 126.
121. Joseph Fitzer, in Günther, "Letter on Human Knowledge," 136.
122. Reardon, *Religion in Romanticism*, 126–27.

to be the decision to establish a philosophical system on the basis of concepts rather than ideas.[123] The effort to avoid this error is evident in Günther's anthropology and cognitional theory, which Vincelette sums up as follows:

> The human self is a unity composed of both a soul (*Seele*) and a spirit (*Geist*) with their various faculties. The soul for its part engages in sensation, imagination, memory, and conceptual thought (*Verstand*); in so doing it structures the appearances of phenomena according to the a priori Kantian categorical concepts (*Begriff*) [as the soul makes use of abstract conceptual thought, it only grasps appearances and not the essence of being]. The spirit (or mind) on the other hand engages in understanding (passive receptivity) and willing or loving (active or spontaneous response). The spirit with its intuitive intellection (*Vernunft*) grasps ideas (*Idee*) and in this way knows the essences of beings, i.e., the ground of appearances.[124]

The glorification of *Vernunft* at the expense of *Verstand* on display here extends into Günther's approach to apologetics. Günther wants to demonstrate "the fundamental truths of Christianity," explains Vincelette, "through the intuitive intelligence or *Vernunft* and not the discursive understanding or *Verstand* which only knows phenomenal appearances."[125] This is perhaps most obvious in Günther's stance on knowledge of God.

The starting point for knowledge of God, for Günther, is human self-consciousness. As Vincelette outlines,

> The spirit with its intuitive intellection (*Vernunft*) . . . grasps the idea of its own being as a free and intellectual self. The human self . . . recognizes that it possesses a body (*Leib*), and lives in a world of nature along with other spirits, although as spirit it is distinct from its body and the natural world. [The human can hence be conceived . . . as . . . a dualistic synthesis of spirit . . . and nature (body and soul).] Moreover, the spirit . . . discerns

---

123. Vincelette, *Recent Catholic Philosophy*, 267n51.
124. Vincelette, *Recent Catholic Philosophy*, 56–57.
125. Vincelette, *Recent Catholic Philosophy*, 56.

that though it is immortal it is still limited and dependent. . . . And reflection on the limited and dependent nature of the spirit gives rise to a knowledge that the human being is created by an infinite and unlimited being, God.[126]

It is what the faculty of *Vernunft* can do once it has obtained this knowledge of God that lands Günther under the umbrella of rationalism. As Vincelette relays, "*Vernunft* . . . can go on to reflect on God's nature and rationally prove truths of Christianity that up to now were only known from faith in revelation (i.e., mysteries of the faith)."[127] For Günther, "the dogmas of the [T]rinity and the [I]ncarnation . . . are fully open to rational comprehension."[128] That said, the nuance of "up to now" in Vincelette's statement is important. There is nothing wrong with those who are "unable to perceive [the Catholic faith's] logical coherence" and "simply . . . 'believe,'" as Reardon puts it, but those who are "capable of philosophical comprehension" will "arrive at knowledge."[129] What is common between the two groups, it must be stressed, is that neither can spontaneously acquire knowledge of the mysteries of faith; one must first learn of them through contact with the Bible. Even among those in the second category who obtain knowledge of the Trinity, such knowledge is not exhaustive. Vincelette elaborates,

> Though reason can show God is triune (why God's nature is the way it is), exactly what it means for God to be triune and how the procession of the Trinity occurs is still mysterious and known by faith alone (i.e., scripturally).[130]

126. Vincelette, *Recent Catholic Philosophy*, 57–58; indentations removed.

127. Vincelette, *Recent Catholic Philosophy*, 58.

128. Reardon, *Religion in Romanticism*, 127.

129. Reardon, *Religion in Romanticism*, 128. Note also Vincelette's comments on Günther's intermittent subscription to the idea of primitive revelation. See Vincelette, *Recent Catholic Philosophy*, 268n56.

130. Vincelette, *Recent Catholic Philosophy*, 61. Günther also deemed *Vernunft* capable of showing that "once God chooses to create the world, God must create a world of nature and spirit" (Vincelette, *Recent Catholic Philosophy*, 58).

What Günther has provided is a way for the "educated classes" to be convinced of the Catholic faith—to see that "it is impossible to hold up the doctrines of the Catholic Church to any reasonable doubt."[131] This apologetic approach is feasible given the correct envisagement of human faculties. As Paul Wenzel sums it up, "The highest objects of faith are assigned to [*Vernunft*]. Only in this way can . . . religion [be] raised to science."[132]

It is clear that the epistemology of *Vernunft* plays a key role in Günther's proofs for both the existence of God and the mysteries of faith, but it is not clear that it is Jacobi's epistemology of *Vernunft* in particular that has been appropriated. To begin to resolve the matter, note that Günther is evidently aware of the background of *Vernunft* and *Verstand*:

> Who does not know what a different place Kant and Jacobi assigned to reason in the system of cognitive forces? According to the former it was the formal capacity for inference, according to the latter a capacity for intuition of the absolute. . . . According to Kant there was not even an indirect knowledge of God and divine things; but according to Jacobi there was . . . an immediate one.[133]

At the end of this quotation, one can already anticipate the basis for Günther's divergence from Jacobi, but the overall relationship is hazy. In *Vorschule zur speculativen Theologie des positiven Christenthums*, Günther writes, "All speculation about God leads to pantheism, as Jacobi has recognized with a true genius's eye."[134] To be sure, there is at least some Jacobian influence in Günther's rejection of discursive arguments for God made via *Verstand*. However, Günther also reproduces criticisms of Jacobi advanced by Gotthold Lessing (d. 1781) and Hegel.[135] In general, the relations

---

131. Reardon, *Religion in Romanticism*, 127–28.
132. Wenzel, *Wissenschaftliche Anliegen des Güntherianismus*, 149.
133. Günther, *Vorschule zur speculativen Theologie*, 1:219.
134. Günther, *Vorschule zur speculativen Theologie*, 2:523.
135. Günther, *Vorschule zur speculativen Theologie*, 2:523.

other "parties" have posited between "reason and understanding" are judged to be unsatisfactory.[136] What specifically leads to Günther's divergence from Jacobi is his view that "[the spirit's] knowledge of itself as conditioned being and limited being" leads to "the idea of unconditional being (God)."[137] Jacobi had asserted that God's existence is simply "revealed to reason."[138]

---

136. Günther, *Vorschule zur speculativen Theologie*, 1:143.
137. Günther and Pabst, *Janusköpfe*, 258.
138. Jacobi, *Main Philosophical Writings*, 583.

2

The Background of *Dei Filius* in Brief

SECTION 1 OF THIS chapter provides a brief overview of magisterial criticism of Bautain and Günther prior to the First Vatican Council. As aimed at figures that represent the two poles of the nineteenth-century debate about faith and reason, such criticism broadly prefigures *Dei Filius*. Section 2 provides a brief timeline of the council and of the composition of *Dei Filius*.

2.1 Magisterial Criticism of Bautain and Günther Before the Council

Seven questions regarding reason's relation to faith were sent to Bautain by the bishop of Strasbourg in 1834.[1] Bautain's replies resulted in an *advertissement* to the clergy of his diocese, the French bishops, and Rome.[2] In the *advertissement*, six of the seven aforementioned questions are posed in a slightly revised form

---

1. These questions (including subsequent revisions and conversions into propositions), as well as Bautain's responses, are reproduced in the original French in Poupard, *Essai de philosophie chrétienne*, 393–96.

2. Régny, *Abbé Bautain*, 213–14. For a more recent account of the ordeal, see B. Long, "Years of Controversy." On the authorship of the *advertissement*, see Livingston, *Modern Christian Thought*, 1:158.

alongside Bautain's original answers. Subsequently, the questions were converted into propositions—receiving revision—and were signed by Bautain in 1835. In 1840 and 1844 Bautain signed further-revised and expanded propositions.[3] Among the issues addressed were the capacity for reason to prove the existence of God, the status of the miracles of Jesus as proofs, and the idea that reason precedes faith and leads to it. Notably, there is fluctuation in the usage of "reason" and "reason alone" in the formulations of items in documents from different years—and even, as Poupard points out, among the propositions in a single document.[4]

In addition to the *advertissement* and its succeeding documents' direct criticism of Bautain, there exists indirect magisterial criticism of his stance. In 1846 Pope Pius IX promulgated *Qui Pluribus*, an encyclical on faith and reason. The encyclical is directed toward philosophers who "boldly prate that it (faith) is repugnant to human reason."[5] If one takes reason to mean discursive reason, which one ought to,[6] elements of the encyclical plainly pertain to Bautain. One especially salient passage reads,

---

3. One finds what is labelled "Theses written by Bautain under order of his bishop, Sept. 8, 1840" in DB 1622-27; DS 2751-57. Since the DB version of Denzinger is widely available, it is referenced here and throughout the present book, but note that if one takes Poupard, *Essai de philosophie chrétienne*, 393-96, to be accurate, then DB contains several errors. No. 1 reads, "is posterior to," but that phrase is from the 1835 document; in 1840, it reads, "presupposes." No. 3 reads, "to those who either reject it or" but again that phrase is from 1835; in 1840, it reads, "to the unbeliever who [*à l'incrédule qui*] rejects it or." No. 4 reads, "the same tradition," but in the 1840 document that phrase is absent. No. 5 should be translated as "reason precedes faith and must [*doit*] lead us to it." Also, note that an English translation of the 1835 document is provided at DB 1627n1, and it appears to be without error.

4. In particular, the 1844 document. See Poupard, *Essai de philosophie chrétienne*, 396n1.

5. DB 1635; DS 2776. Parentheses in the original.

6. One can safely assume that the encyclical follows Aquinas in its usage of the term. As Bruno Niederbacher outlines, "Aquinas usually means with 'reason'—*ratio*—in its wide sense capacities and acts of *natural* human cognition. Natural human cognition starts by sense perception and, through processes of abstraction, ends up by grasping the essences of things. In a narrower sense, 'reason' means cognitive acts of drawing conclusions from

The Background of Dei Filius in Brief

For, even if faith is above reason, nevertheless, no true dissension or disagreement can ever be found between them, since both have their origin from one and the same font of immutable, eternal truth, the excellent and great God, and they mutually help one another so much that right reason demonstrates the truth of faith, protects it, defends it.[7]

As a result of this encyclical, both fideism and traditionalism were, as Vincelette states, "formally condemned."[8]

Turning to magisterial criticism of Günther, in January of 1857, the Congregation of the Index prohibited nine of Günther's works. As noted in chapter 1, Joseph Kleutgen had carried out an examination of the works.[9] Günther accepted the prohibition the following month. The grounds of the prohibition appear in *Eximiam Tuam*, a brief issued by Pope Pius IX in June of that year. The brief is directed towards the "erroneous and most dangerous system of rationalism" found in Günther's works.[10] It rejects his human anthropology and laments that he attributes "the rights of a master both to human reason and philosophy, whereas they should be wholly handmaids, not masters in religious matters."[11] Pope Pius IX's apostolic letter *Dolore Haud Mediocri*, written in April of 1860, once again deems Günther's human anthropology erroneous.[12] Finally, there exists in the Vatican Archives a document entitled *Brevis Synopsis Errorum, Qui Leguntur in Scriptis Antonii Günther* (Brief synopsis of the

---

premises or finding premises for conclusions" (Niederbacher, "Relation of Reason," 339–40; emphasis in original).

7. DB 1635; DS 2776.

8. Vincelette, *Recent Catholic Philosophy*, 46.

9. Inglis, *Spheres of Philosophical Inquiry*, 78, 80. McCool relays that in Kleutgen's *Die Theologie der Vorzeit* (in particular, the fourth tractatus of the first volume), Günther is not named but his theology is criticized—and that volume was published the same year Günther's works were placed on the index (McCool, *Nineteenth-Century Scholasticism*, 278n60).

10. DB 1655; DS 2828.

11. DB 1656; DS 2829.

12. A portion of the letter is reproduced in DB 1655n3.

errors in the works of Anton Günther), which as McCool notes was discovered by Paul Wenzel.[13]

Indirect magisterial criticism of Günther is found in the 1863 apostolic letter *Tuas Libenter*. In it Pope Pius IX rejects a "recent and preposterous method of philosophizing."[14] Not naming Günther but unmistakably pertaining to him, the letter states that "human reason . . . can never be made fit to understand or demonstrate [mysteries of faith] by its own powers, and on its own natural principles."[15] It should be noted that whereas reason referred to discursive reason above, in the criticism of Bautain, it appears to be used more generally. Otherwise, it would be the case that Günther is not blameworthy, for he rejects *Verstand*'s capacity to arrive at knowledge of the mysteries.

The encyclical *Quanta Cura*, promulgated by Pope Pius IX in 1864, was accompanied by the document *Syllabus Errorum*. Parts of the section entitled "Modified Rationalism" apply to Günther, especially insofar as they echo *Tuas Libenter*. The document deems erroneous the notions that "theological studies must be conducted just as the philosophical," that "dogmas . . . are the object of natural science or philosophy," and that "the method and principles according to which the ancient scholastic doctors treated theology are by no means suited to the necessities of our times and to the progress of the sciences."[16]

2.2 Timeline of the Council and the Composition of *Dei Filius*

In December of 1864, at a meeting of the Congregation of Rites, Pope Pius IX privately informed the cardinals present that he

---

13. McCool, *Nineteenth-Century Scholasticism*, 278n60. The document is reproduced in Wenzel, *Wissenschaftliche Anliegen des Güntherianismus*, 248–54.

14. DB 1682; DS 2878.

15. DB 1682; DS 2878.

16. DB 1708–9, 1713; DS 2908–9, 2913.

intended to hold an ecumenical council.[17] In March of 1865, he appointed a central commission tasked with preparing for the council. In April of that year, a letter was sent to a select group of bishops asking them to specify issues that should be addressed at the council. The issues related to the relationship between faith and reason that appear in their responses are as follows: pantheism, naturalism, rationalism, socialism, communism, spiritism, and religious indifference.[18]

Based on all of the responses of the bishops, five subsidiary commissions were established: faith and dogma; ecclesiastical discipline and canon law; religious order and regulars; oriental churches and foreign missions; politico-ecclesiastical affairs and relations of the church and state.[19] These commissions were tasked with composing schemata (draft constitutions). Due to the war between Austria and Prussia, they were stalled until 1867.[20] In what follows, the faith and dogma commission is of exclusive interest, for it is the commission that goes on to compose the constitution that this chapter and chapter 3 focus on.

In September of 1867, the faith and dogma commission adopted Pope Pius IX's 1864 encyclical *Quanta Cura* and the accompanying *Syllabus Errorum* as its primary guide.[21] Pope Pius IX then selected December 8, 1869, as the date of the opening of the council. In the meantime, *votum* discussions would take place. A *votum* is a document that outlines issues to be addressed in a schema. In August of 1868, theological consultor John Baptist Franzelin (d. 1886) submitted a 143-page *votum*.[22] The evolution

17. Butler, *Vatican Council*, 63. For a short, chronological list of events, see Aubert, *Vatican I*, 323–24. For extensive discussion of the development of the constitution, see Pottmeyer, *Glaube*; Schatz, *Vaticanum I*, vol. 2. On the historical context of the council, see "The Church in a State of Siege, AD 1650–1891," pt. 4, in Bokenkotter, *Concise History*.

18. Butler, *Vatican Council*, 65.

19. Butler, *Vatican Council*, 70.

20. Butler, *Vatican Council*, 65.

21. Hennesey, "Vatican Council I," 14:404. See also Granderath, *Concile du Vatican*, 2.2:12.

22. "De erroribus nonnullis circa cognitionem naturalem et supernaturalem

of this document over the ensuing twelve months is essential to the history of the constitution. Franzelin was asked to revise the 143-page *votum* and render it in the form of a schema. In response, Franzelin submitted a ten-chapter schema, which Hermann-Josef Pottmeyer refers to as Schema I.[23] Asked to revise it, Franzelin submitted an eighteen-chapter schema, which Pottmeyer refers to as Schema II.[24] It would be several months before this schema would undergo debate at the council.

Council participants began to gather in Rome in November of 1869.[25] There would be three kinds of sessions at the council: private sessions for discussing schemata, general congregations (primarily) for deciding whether or not a schema is acceptable, and public sessions for the promulgation of an accepted schema.[26] At the first general congregation, held December 10, 1869, a total of 679 participants were in attendance: 43 cardinals, 605 bishops, and 31 abbots and generals of religious orders.[27]

General debate of Schema II began December 28, 1869.[28] If found unacceptable, it would undergo revision by the deputation on faith, a group of twenty-four fathers established earlier in December.[29] In early January of 1870, Schema II was in fact

---

seu circa habitudinem inter scientiam ac fidem qui nostra aetate scholis catholicis periculum crearunt," in Pottmeyer, *Glaube*, 28*–89*. For a discussion of this *votum*, which includes a list of theologians and works referenced, see Pottmeyer, *Glaube*, 472–76.

23. "Definitio doctrinae catholicae contra multiplices errores ex impio rationalismo derivatos vel contra multiplices absoluti ac temperati rationalismi errores," in Pottmeyer, *Glaube*, 90*–105*.

24. "Schema constitutionis dogmaticae de doctrina catholica contra multiplices errores ex rationalismo derivatos patrum examini propositum," in Mansi, *Sacrorum Conciliorum*, 50:59–74. For a side-by-side comparison of the titles of ten chapters of Schema I and Schema II, see Pottmeyer, *Glaube*, 477.

25. Butler, *Vatican Council*, 108.
26. Butler, *Vatican Council*, 131.
27. Butler, *Vatican Council*, 138.
28. Butler, *Vatican Council*, 158–59.
29. Butler, *Vatican Council*, 148.

deemed unacceptable and therefore sent to the deputation on faith.[30] The deputation "resolved with unanimity that [Schema II] should be retained in substance, but emended: it should be shortened, and made more clear; its tone should be tranquil, . . . and all the harshness of expression eliminated."[31] Three members of the deputation were chosen to carry out the emendations: Victor Auguste Dechamps, Louis François Désiré Pie, and Konrad Martin.[32] Martin, the head of the group, asked for the assistance of two theologians: Joseph Kleutgen and Charles Louis Gay.[33]

Before the end of February 1870, Martin was in possession of a nine-chapter schema, which Pottmeyer refers to as Schema III.[34] Kleutgen was its "main author."[35] On March 1, 1870, the schema was laid before the deputation on faith; its first four chapters dealt with fundamental issues, while its remaining chapters dealt with particular doctrines.[36]

On March 14, 1870, a four-chapter schema was circulated among the fathers, which is referred to by Pottmeyer as Schema IV.[37] General debate of it commenced on March 18. Ultimately, the remainder of Kleutgen's nine-chapter schema did not go before the council.[38]

Further amendments were made to each chapter of Schema IV,[39] but finally, with a *placet* (approval) vote by all 677 fathers

30. Butler, *Vatican Council*, 159.

31. Butler, *Vatican Council*, 169. These are Butler's words, not those of council participants.

32. Butler, *Vatican Council*, 170.

33. Butler, *Vatican Council*, 170.

34. "Schema reformatum constitutionis dogmaticae de fide catholica patrum deputatorum examini propositum," in Mansi, *Sacrorum Conciliorum*, 53:164–77.

35. Schatz, *Vaticanum I*, 2:314. The same attribution can be found in Granderath, *Concile du Vatican*, 2.2:12.

36. Butler, *Vatican Council*, 235.

37. "Schema reformatum constitutionis dogmaticae de fide catholica patrum examini propositum," in Mansi, *Sacrorum Conciliorum*, 51:31–38.

38. Butler, *Vatican Council*, 235.

39. Butler, *Vatican Council*, 241–42. The revisions made can be seen in

present on April 24, 1870,[40] the council promulgated the *Dogmatic Constitution on the Catholic Faith (Dei Filius)*.[41]

On July 18, 1870, the council promulgated a second document, the *First Dogmatic Constitution on the Church of Christ (Pastor Aeternus)*.[42] Discussions of other schemata followed but were impeded by the withdrawal of French troops from Rome in August and the occupation of Vatican City by Italian troops in September.[43] In an apostolic letter dated October 20, 1870, Pope Pius IX suspended the council.

Vacant, *Études théologiques*, 1:678–95; 2:341–57.

40. Butler, *Vatican Council*, 247.

41. *Constitutio dogmatica de fide catholica*, in Mansi, *Sacrorum Conciliorum*, 51:429–36.

42. *Constitutio dogmatica prima de ecclesia Christi*, in Mansi, *Sacrorum Conciliorum*, 52:1330–34.

43. Butler, *Vatican Council*, 416.

3

Faith and Reason in *Dei Filius*

WITH THE BACKGROUND OF the constitution having been sketched in the preceding chapter, its content can now be examined. In what follows, key statements in each of the four chapters of *Dei Filius* will be discussed.[1] Key statements are those with a bearing on the relationship between faith and reason. The discussion throughout this chapter is informed by what was explored in chapter 1 of this book.

Four things should be noted in advance. First, *Dei Filius* will henceforth be referred to as the constitution. Second, English-language quotations of the constitution will be from *The Sources of Catholic Dogma* (DB), unless otherwise noted.[2] Third, Latin-language quotations of the constitution will be exclusively from Mansi's *Sacrorum Conciliorum*.[3] Fourth, the 1963 publication of *Enchiridion Symbolorum* (DS) has been, and will continue to be, utilized to provide Denzinger-Schönmetzer numbers.

---

1. Note that the preface of the constitution will not be examined. As Jared Wicks observes, the preface "is not part of the official teaching of Vatican Council I on revelation and faith" (*Doing Theology*, 266n3).

2. DB 1781–820; DS 3000–3043.

3. Namely, Mansi, *Sacrorum Conciliorum*, 51:429–36.

3.1 Chapter 1 of the Constitution: God, Creator of All Things

Chapter 1 of the constitution treats the distinction between God and creation. As such, it does not contain any statements that directly address the relationship between faith and reason. However, the function of one of its statements is worth clarifying. The statement reads,

> The holy, Catholic, Apostolic, Roman Church believes and confesses that there is one, true, living God, Creator and Lord of heaven and earth, omnipotent, eternal, immense, incomprehensible, infinite in intellect and will, and in every perfection; who, although He is one, singular, altogether simple and unchangeable spiritual substance, must be proclaimed distinct in reality and essence from the world; most blessed in Himself and of Himself, and ineffably most high above all things which are or can be conceived outside Himself [can. 1–4].[4]

What this statement contains is an "enumeration of the various attributes that denote the true God," according to Réginald Garrigou-Lagrange. He continues, "It was not the intention of the Council to define as a dogma of faith that all these attributes can be proved by reason alone."[5]

3.2 Chapter 2 of the Constitution: Revelation

Chapter 2 contains the constitution's most well-known statement. While the statement itself does not explicitly pertain to revelation, what immediately follows it does pertain to that topic. Normally, this would call for a consideration of both the statement and what follows it, but given the gravity of the statement itself, it will be considered on its own first. The statement reads,

---

4. DB 1782; DS 3001. Bracketed references that are present in DB, such as [can. 1–4], are retained here and beyond.

5. Garrigou-Lagrange, *God*, 1:14.

Faith and Reason in Dei Filius

> The same Holy Mother Church holds and teaches that God, the beginning and end of all things, can be known with certitude by the natural light of human reason from created things; "for the invisible things of him, from the creation of the world, are clearly seen, being understood by the things that are made" [Rom 1:20].[6]

There is much to unpack in this statement. Insight into it and many others can be gained through Bishop Vincent Gasser (d. 1879), the *rapporteur* of the deputation on faith. According to a *relatio* (report) by Gasser, the statement above "deal[s] only with man in general" and "is only about the power, certainly not merely passive but active, of knowing God."[7] More will be said about this in due course. At present, simply note that one must be cautious in interpreting the constitution, for words as unassuming as "can" have tremendous weight.

The phrase "the beginning and end of all things" was objected to by one of the fathers of the council on the ground that "neither Aristotle, nor Plato, nor Tullius, who demonstrated almost all the power of reason, . . . could know with certainty that God is the beginning and end of all things."[8] But as Ambrose Ryan explains, the phrase aims to communicate that "human reason can, by its own light, establish an essentially correct notion of the true God . . . [and] that in so doing the human mind acknowledges the existence of God."[9]

Curiously, the fathers do not include what follows the phrase "the invisible things of him" in the Vulgate, namely, the specification of "eternal power . . . and divinity."[10] Nonetheless, the fathers

---

6. DB 1785; DS 3004.

7. Granderath, *Acta et Decreta*, 236. Latin: "Agi in hoc capite solummodo de homine in genere, quidquid sit de singulis; agi solummodo de potentia, utique non mere passiva sed activa, Deum lumine naturali certo cognoscendi."

8. Granderath, *Acta et Decreta*, 224. Latin: "Neque Aristoteles, neque Plato, neque Tullius, qui fere omnem rationis potentiam praemonstrarunt, . . . potuerunt cum certitudine cognoscere Deum principium et finem omnium rerum."

9. Ryan, "Knowledge of God," 366.

10. In the Vulgate, the verse in full reads, "Invisibilia enim ipsius a creatura

retain the plural, "the invisible things of him," expressing that more than just the existence of God can be known. The exclusion of specification might stem from the statement aiming to be "only about the power" of reason. Also excluded, and perhaps for the same reason, is the ensuing verse in Romans, which goes beyond power to actual achievement: "for though they knew God" (Rom 1:21). These exclusions also represent a scale-down from an oft-quoted claim by Aquinas: "That God exists, that He is one, and the like . . . have been proved demonstratively by the philosophers, guided by the light of the natural reason."[11]

Another purpose of the phrase "the beginning and end of all things," as revealed in a *relatio* by Gasser, is to communicate that "it is possible for man to understand and know the most important moral duties."[12] Among these, writes George Smith, are "duties of worship, love and thanksgiving"—and "[man's] duties to himself and to his fellow men."[13] The phrase also serves to counter deists, according to Marcel Chossat. For the fathers, natural knowledge of God "is such that it makes possible the beginning of the moral and religious life."[14]

To say that a person can know God, can know his or her moral obligations to God, and can know divine attributes, is plainly a substantial claim. Nevertheless, it should not distract from the meagerness of the statement. In addition to speaking only of potential, the constitution makes no reference to arguments for the existence of God. One would not be unjustified in thinking that

---

mundi per ea quae facta sunt intellecta conspiciuntur sempiterna quoque eius et virtus et divinitas ut sint inexcusabiles" (Rom 1:20).

11. Aquinas, *Summa Contra Gentiles*, 1:63, I.3.2.

12. Granderath, *Acta et Decreta*, 133. Latin: "Posse hominem intelligere et cognoscere officia principaliora moralia." Because the phrase communicates this, a reference to natural law at this juncture would be "superfluous" (133).

13. George Smith, "Faith and Revealed Truth," 4. A canon later in the constitution contains the phrase "natural knowledge of God and moral things." See DB 1811; DS 3032.

14. Chossat, "Dieu (Connaissance naturelle de)," 4.1:838. Attention is drawn to this dictionary entry in Kerr, "Knowing God by Reason," 220.

the Five Ways,[15] for example, might receive mention as a means by which one could know God via the natural light of reason. Nonetheless, the fathers avoid particulars, positing only "the power to obtain knowledge of the true God," as Ryan puts it.[16]

Though it speaks only of a power, the statement has proscriptive force. The most obvious of the proscribed positions is traditionalism, which holds that reason, no matter how it is conceived of, lacks the power to know God. One would also expect fideism to be proscribed, since Bautain is referred to by name in Franzelin's *votum*.[17] The phrase that effects the proscription is "natural light," as Ryan observes.[18] For Bautain, one can know that God exists through *l'intelligence* but not without the action of the Eternal Light communicating truth.[19]

Additional targets of the statement can be ascertained through Gasser. He reveals a concern about the opinion, widespread since the "encyclopedists of Gaul" and "critical philosophy in Germany," that "the existence of God cannot be proved with absolute certainty by certain arguments."[20] The phrase "with certitude" can thus be interpreted as countering thinkers who hold, like the encyclopedists, that God's existence is probable—or, like critical philosophy, that God's existence is a practical postulate. Both positions allow for "knowledge" of God through reason but the degree of that "knowledge" is less than certain. The phrase was also chosen for its tone. Gasser relays the rationale:

---

15. Aquinas, *Summa Theologica*, 1:13, I, q. 2, a. 3.
16. Ryan, "Knowledge of God," 366.
17. Pottmeyer, *Glaube*, 473.
18. Ryan, "Knowledge of God," 367.

19. Horton, *Philosophy of Abbé Bautain*, 151. It is worth registering that when Bautain's or Günther's views are said to be proscribed by the constitution, it is their views as expressed in their major writings, which continued to influence theologians up to the time of the council.

20. Granderath, *Acta et Decreta*, 130. Latin: "Nostis enim . . . quaenam opinio invaluerit in animis multorum hominum inde a sic dictis encyclopaedistis Galliae, et inde ab initio philosophiae criticae in Germania: . . . existentiam Dei omnino certo non posse probari certis argumentis."

> Although in some measure *to know with certitude* and *to demonstrate* are one and the same, the deputation on faith nevertheless resolved to select the milder phrase rather than the more demanding one.[21]

It is important not to misinterpret the decision to move away from the word "demonstrate."[22] Recall from chapter 1 of this book that Kleutgen saw it necessary to compare the faculties of *Vernunft* and *Verstand* with what he took to be their Scholastic alternatives: *intellectus* (understanding) and *ratio* (reason).[23] And recall that, as Aquinas articulates, "*intellectus* takes its name from being an intimate penetration of the truth, while *ratio* is so called from being inquisitive and discursive."[24] According to Alfred Vacant, *ratio* in the statement on natural knowledge of God stands for both *intellectus* and *ratio*, but the fathers invoke *ratio* alone in order to establish a contrast with faith, which "submits to the truth without arguing or reasoning."[25] When one couples this decision with the statement's designation of natural knowledge of God as coming through a medium (namely, created things), overexaggerating the departure from "demonstrate" is a risk. Garrigou-Lagrange asks, "What else is a certain and mediate knowledge acquired by reasoning, but a demonstration?"[26] Nevertheless, the word is not present in the constitution and thus not a required belief.

---

21. Granderath, *Acta et Decreta*, 132; emphasis in original; "deputation" set in lowercase for consistency. Latin: "Quamvis aliquatenus *certo cognoscere* et *demonstrare* sit unum idemque, tamen phrasim mitiorem Deputatio de fide sibi eligendam censuit, et non istam duriorem."

22. When it was present, the fathers would have used the term "demonstration" the same way Aquinas does: "An argument with evidently true premises that entail its conclusion" (Davies, *Thomas Aquinas's "Summa,"* 23).

23. Kleutgen, *Philosophie der Vorzeit*, 1:234, §145.

24. Aquinas, *Summa Theologica*, 2:1404, II-II, q. 49, a. 5, ad. 3.

25. Vacant, *Études théologiques*, 1:291.

26. Garrigou-Lagrange, *God*, 1:23. While taking Garrigou-Lagrange's point, it can also be stated that by not invoking the term "demonstration," the fathers do not have to address certain technicalities, such as the distinction between demonstration *quia* and demonstration *propter quid*. On this distinction, see Davies, *Thomas Aquinas's "Summa,"* 24–25.

Given that "can," "know," "with certitude," and "reason" are charged expressions in the constitution, one can expect "from created things" to follow suit. To know God in this way, relays Gasser, is to know God "through the traces which are impressed upon all creatures"—and this does not "exclude the image which is imprinted on the immortal soul of man."[27] That the fathers are open to the image of God in human beings, described in Gen 1:26–27, as a medium for knowledge of God is noteworthy. It can be assumed that the fathers uphold Aquinas's association of the image of God with the human capacities to understand and to love.[28] The created things that knowledge of God through reason is mediated by, then, are not for the fathers exclusively physical things outside of the human being. In fact, as Ryan indicates, the fathers consciously chose not to condemn Anselm's (d. 1109) ontological argument, nor innatism and ontologism.[29]

The absence of condemnation should not, of course, be taken as endorsement. For example, the fathers view the proposition "Direct and immediate knowledge of God is natural to man" as central to ontologism and "the foundation of many errors which have now spread widely."[30] In the end, though, the fathers judged it better to address this -ism elsewhere, rather than "perfunctorily" in the constitution.[31]

The question arises here as to whether Günther's view of knowledge of God is proscribed in the constitution. Although

---

27. Granderath, *Acta et Decreta*, 132. Latin: "Per vestigia quae creaturis omnibus impressa sunt; multo minus excludimus imaginem, quae animae hominis immortali impressa est."

28. Aquinas writes, "Since man is said to be the image of God by reason of his intellectual nature, he is the most perfectly like God according to that in which he can best imitate God in his intellectual nature. Now the intellectual nature imitates God chiefly in this, that God understands and loves Himself" (Aquinas, *Summa Theologica*, 1:471, I, q. 93, a. 4, co.).

29. Ryan, "Knowledge of God," 372.

30. Granderath, *Acta et Decreta*, 849. Latin: "Fundamentum est multorum errorum, qui nunc late pervagati sunt: et continetur illa propositione: 'Naturalis est homini cognitio Dei directa et immediata.'"

31. Granderath, *Acta et Decreta*, 849. Latin: *perfunctorie*.

Günther is referred to in Franzelin's *votum*,[32] it seems the problematic aspect of his writings rests outside of knowledge of God. For Günther, "[The spirit's] knowledge about itself as a conditioned being"[33] is a necessary step in grasping the reality of God. Günther thus evades the charge of direct knowledge of God that the fathers expressed concern about above.

Chapter 2 of the constitution, to reiterate, is entitled "Revelation." Given what has been considered thus far, it seems unfitting. This changes when one reads what immediately follows the statement that God can be known with certitude by the natural light of human reason from created things:

> Nevertheless, it has pleased His wisdom and goodness to reveal Himself and the eternal decrees of His will to the human race in another and supernatural way, as the Apostle says: "God, who at sundry times and in divers manners, spoke in times past to the fathers by the prophets, last of all, in these days hath spoken to us by His Son" [Heb 1:1–2; can. 1].[34]

René Latourelle explains that through the statement above and the one previously considered, "the Council distinguishes two ways by which man can arrive at knowledge of God: the ascendant way of natural knowledge, and the descendent way of revelation."[35] Although this chapter endeavors not to leap forward in the constitution, it is prudent to do so here. Latourelle delineates what the statement above advances as knowable, from the standpoint of the end of the constitution. He writes,

> The ... object of revelation is God Himself and the eternal decrees of His free will. ... By the word *God*, we must understand His existence, His attributes, as well as the intimate life of the three Persons [of the Trinity]. And

---

32. Pottmeyer, *Glaube*, 473–76.

33. Günther and Pabst, *Janusköpfe*, 258.

34. DB 1785; DS 3004. That the statement employs only the words "spoke" and "spoken" does not, of course, exclude God's deeds in history as a manner in which God has revealed himself.

35. Latourelle, *Theology of Revelation*, 259.

by the word *decrees*, we must understand those which concern the creation and natural government of the world, as well as those which concern our elevation to the supernatural order[:] the Incarnation, Redemption, call of the elect.[36]

What this delineation brings to light are the points of overlap between the ascendant way and the descendent way, namely, God's existence and God's attributes. In the statement, the phrase "another and supernatural way" communicates that these items have already been revealed but are concomitantly offered in a way that is supernatural. Still, caution is needed in conceiving the first way as revelation. As Smith explains,

> It is true to say that God "speaks" to us in the works of nature, inasmuch as those works "reveal" his presence and activity; it is true, but it is metaphorical. Revelation properly understood . . . [means] God truly speaks—i.e., makes an assertion, which man accepts on God's personal authority.[37]

Smith's explanation clarifies the status of "another and supernatural way" but also wades into a matter not yet addressed in the constitution: God's authority.

Before proceeding to the next salient statement in chapter 2, the canon pertaining to the statement on knowledge of God through reason must be discussed. It reads,

> If anyone shall have said that the one true God, our Creator and our Lord, cannot be known with certitude by those things which have been made, by the natural light of human reason: let him be anathema.[38]

One way of gaining insight into the intention behind this canon is to contrast its iteration in the constitution with that found in Schema III. The core of the canon in Schema III reads, "known with certitude and demonstrated by fallen man [through] those things

---

36. Latourelle, *Theology of Revelation*, 260; emphasis in original.
37. George Smith, "Faith and Revealed Truth," 7; emphasis in original.
38. DB 1806; DS 3026.

which have been made, by natural reason."³⁹ Two of the changes made to this iteration echo above-discussed stances taken by the fathers. Abandoning "demonstrated" echoes the decision "to select the milder phrase ['known with certitude']." And abandoning "by fallen man" echoes the decision to "deal only with man in general." The third change made is the introduction of "natural light" into the canon. With this present, but with "fallen man" absent, there is no specification of the state of a human's reason that has the power to acquire knowledge of God.

The question arises as to whether a specification was perhaps envisioned by the fathers but not declared. It is best to leave this matter to the second last section of chapter 4 of this book, where Lonergan's comments on the removal of "fallen man" will be evaluated. It is also the case that this chapter primarily attends to what the constitution *does* say; the equally important topic of what it does not say will be addressed in the last sections of chapter 4 and chapter 5.

Also noteworthy regarding the canon was the suggested removal of "our Creator and our Lord" for exaggerating the scope of what ancient Greek philosophers, for example, were able to know about God. It was acknowledged that the scope is debated but "at least they were able to know God the creator."⁴⁰ As Chossat elaborates,

> It is defined [in the constitution] that reason can know the God who is creator in the broad sense of the word, but it is not defined that by reason alone, independently of any revelation, one can know him with certainty *as* creator *in the strict sense*.⁴¹

---

39. Mansi, *Sacrorum Conciliorum*, 53:168. Latin: "Si quis negaverit, Deum unum et verum, creatorem et Dominum nostrum, per ea, quae facta sunt, naturali ratione ab homine lapso certo cognosci et demonstrari posse; anathema sit." See also Mansi, *Sacrorum Conciliorum*, 50:76–77.

40. Granderath, *Acta et Decreta*, 243. Latin: "Saltem potuerint cognoscere Deum creatorem."

41. Chossat, "Dieu (Connaissance naturelle de)," 4.1:837; emphasis in original.

This is a reiteration of the earlier point about the attainability of an essentially correct notion of God. Thus the fathers, as Vacant sums it up,

> did not intend to condemn as a heretic, a man who would challenge reason's power to show with certainty the attributes which the canon enumerates; they condemned only men who would refuse to reason sufficient light to know the true God.[42]

The term "Creator" was retained also on the ground of its appearance in the Wisdom of Solomon.[43] Finally, an observation attached to Schema IV deems *a creatura mundi* (Rom 1:20) a basis for using the word Creator.[44]

Another salient statement in chapter 2 explains why overlap between the ascendant and descendent ways of knowing God is beneficial for human beings. It is prudent here to use an alternate translation, signaled by brackets, for part of the statement:

> Indeed, it must be attributed to this divine revelation [that those matters concerning God which are not of themselves beyond the scope of human reason] can, even in this present condition of the human race, be known readily by all with firm certitude and with no admixture of error. Nevertheless, it is not for this reason that revelation is said to be absolutely necessary, but because God in His infinite goodness has ordained man for a supernatural end, to participation, namely, in the divine goods which altogether surpass the understanding of the human mind, since "eye hath not seen, nor ear heard, neither hath it entered into the heart of man, what things God hath prepared for them that love Him" [1 Cor 2:9; can. 2 and 3].[45]

---

42. Vacant, *Études théologiques*, 1:309.

43. Granderath, *Acta et Decreta*, 243. More specifically: "For from the greatness and beauty of created things comes a corresponding perception of their Creator" (Wis 13:5).

44. Mansi, *Sacrorum Conciliorum*, 51:39–40.

45. DB 1786; DS 3005. The alternate translation in brackets is from Tanner, *Decrees of Ecumenical Councils*, 2:806. It is worth noting that Schema I and

Whereas a previous statement merely established that there is an ascendant and descendent way of knowing God, this statement shows how their character differs. Recall that the ascendant way was treated as a possibility. The descendent way, by contrast, is said above to be available in the "present condition of the human race," and it is adorned with expressions such as "readily," "by all," "firm certitude," and "no . . . error."[46]

The statement above goes on to clarify that these provisions, which specifically apply to those truths that overlap the ascendant and descendent fields, are not what made revelation absolutely necessary. Recall that for Bautain, as Latourelle expresses, "revelation . . . is absolutely necessary to know the truths of natural religion."[47] While not directly correcting Bautain, the statement above moves attention away from his concentration, namely, the unsteadiness of reason. Instead, the statement directs attention toward God's plan, referred to in 1 Cor 2:9—the plan for human "participation . . . in . . . divine goods." That is the locus of the necessity of revelation. As Latourelle elaborates,

> Since God has assigned man a supernatural end, [H]e must, if He means to respect the intelligence and free nature of man, make him know this end and the means which will assure its possession: He must reveal them to him. It is thus, in the last analysis, the salvific will of God which explains the necessary character of revelation of the truths of the supernatural order.[48]

Schema II contain further specification: those matters concerning God *and the natural law* that are not of themselves beyond the scope of human reason. See Pottmeyer, *Glaube*, 94*; Mansi, *Sacrorum Conciliorum*, 50:62. The disappearance of the specification in subsequent schemata coincides with the earlier judgment that what the phrase "God, the beginning and end of all things" communicates to us makes a reference to natural law "superfluous." Perhaps it was also judged that readers of the constitution would be aware of the content of Rom 2:14.

46. These expressions are drawn from Aquinas, *Summa Contra Gentiles*, 1:66–68, I.4.3–5.

47. Latourelle, *Theology of Revelation*, 257.

48. Latourelle, *Theology of Revelation*, 261; the first "he" is lowercase in the original.

Latourelle's explanation highlights one of two respects in which the plan of salvation "surpasses human understanding," namely, it could not have been discovered without being revealed by God. To be clear, even perfectly functioning understanding could not, in this life, discover the divine plan.[49]

A second respect, namely, the plan continues to exceed our intellects once revealed, was submitted for inclusion in the constitution but not ultimately used.[50] In its absence, the position of Günther is not condemned. His position, summed up by Latourelle, is as follows: "Once ... in possession of the formulas of faith, man can penetrate their secret and scientifically demonstrate their truth."[51] It will not be until chapter 4—when the fathers invoke the term "mysteries" and posit a canon in relation to them—that a correction will occur.

3.3 Chapter 3 of the Constitution: Faith

In chapter 3 of the constitution, there is for the first time an invocation of faith in conjunction with reason:

> Since man is wholly dependent on God as his Creator and Lord, and since created reason is completely subject to uncreated truth, we are bound by faith to give full obedience of intellect and will to God who reveals [can. 1]. But the Catholic Church professes that this faith, which "is the beginning of human salvation" [cf. n. 801], is a supernatural virtue by which we, with the aid and inspiration of the grace of God, believe that the things revealed by Him are true, not because the intrinsic truth of the revealed things has been perceived by the natural

---

49. More specifically: "God's plan is that mankind, through Christ, Incarnate Word, approach the Father in the Spirit and become sharers in the divine nature. The divine plan ... includes the three principal mysteries of Christianity: Trinity, Incarnation, Grace" (Latourelle, *Theology of Revelation*, 459). And "mysteries are ... truths of which only God possesses a natural knowledge" (264).

50. Guarino, "Vatican I," 77.

51. Latourelle, *Theology of Revelation*, 257.

light of reason, but because of the authority of God Himself who reveals them, who can neither deceive nor be deceived [can. 2]. For, "faith is," as the Apostle testifies, "the substance of things to be hoped for, the evidence of things that appear not" [Heb 11:1].⁵²

The expression "by which . . . we believe that," it is worth noting, is rooted in a long-standing distinction. Augustine, for example, distinguished between *fides qua creditur* (the faith by which [something] is believed) and *fides quae creditur* (the faith which is believed).⁵³ Also long-standing is the portrayal of the relationship between faith and reason against the backdrop of the relationship between God and humankind. As Latourelle observes, "Creation is the basis for the homage of intelligence and will which man owes to God; *created* reason must bow before *uncreated* Truth."⁵⁴ Grasping the character of that bow is essential to understanding the constitution as a whole.

The bow to uncreated truth, the statement clarifies, involves both intellect and will. The role that these faculties play in relation to faith is elucidated by Smith:

> Revealed truth is not seen in itself; it is seen as credible, as clothed, so to speak, in the garment of divine authority. Invested with such authority, it becomes indeed a fit object for intellectual acceptance; but the intellect alone, eager to "read within" (*intus legere*) the truth, makes no spontaneous move to accept it. It is here that the intervention of the will becomes necessary. . . . The mind sees the revealed truth as credible, and the will bends the mind to accept it. . . . And the motive of the act is the authority of God who attests to that truth. This motive . . . is one which appeals to both mind and will. . . . To the mind it appeals as endowing the statement with credibility; to the will it appeals as a divine perfection to be worshipped.⁵⁵

---

52. DB 1789; DS 3008.
53. Augustine of Hippo, *Trinity*, 375, §13.2.
54. Latourelle, *Theology of Revelation*, 262; emphasis in original.
55. George Smith, "Faith and Revealed Truth," 19. The view of Louis Billot

Faith and Reason in Dei Filius

If the significance of the authority of God attesting to revealed truth rests, for the believer, in the fact that God is omniscient (the fact that God can neither deceive nor be deceived), it must be asked: What role, if any, is played by knowledge of that fact? Smith answers,

> The believer accepts a revealed truth not precisely *because he knows* that God has revealed it and *knows* that God is infallible. This knowledge is the necessary condition, but it is not the motive, of his faith. He believes because *God*, who is infallible, has said it. The difference is perhaps subtle, but it is important. The motive of the act of divine faith is not *my knowledge* of that authority as accrediting revealed truth, however certain, however evident that knowledge may be, but the divine authority itself. My knowledge is finite, my knowledge is fallible. God's authority is infinite; God can neither deceive nor be deceived. . . . Hence the firmness of my assent is measured not by the cogency of any one, or indeed of the sum, of the reasons which led me to judge the truth as credible.[56]

Bracketing the specifics of the judgment of credibility, what must be grasped here is the fact that no argument, whether it is made within *Verstand*, *Vernunft*, or some other faculty, changes the firmness of the assent of faith itself.

The phrase "with the aid and inspiration of the grace of God" in the statement presents a third component of faith—the first two being the obedience of the intellect and the obedience of the will. Such aid and inspiration are needed to assent even with the created status of reason warranting a bow to uncreated truth. With respect to the lead-up to the assent, the constitution does not say whether the aid and inspiration of grace is involved. This point will be returned to shortly. At present, it can simply be stressed that even when the aid and inspiration of grace are involved in the lead-up

---

(d. 1931), summed up by Dulles, helpfully puts the same point in different words: faith is free "because the mind cannot assent out of reverence except under the influence of the will," yet it is also "absolutely certain because the firmness of the assent is proportionate to the dignity of the witness, which is the motive" (Dulles, *Assurance*, 105).

56. George Smith, "Faith and Revealed Truth," 21–23.

to faith, they are not coercive, just as such aid and inspiration are not coercive in the assent of faith itself. For the council fathers, Dulles stresses, "the decision of faith . . . is a truly free and personal response to a call that comes from on high."[57]

Chapter 3 goes on to claim that the Holy Spirit works with reason in the context of accepting revelation:

> [In order that the submission of our faith should be in accordance with reason,] God has willed that to the internal aids of the Holy Spirit there should be joined external proofs of His revelation, namely: [divine acts], especially miracles and prophecies which, because they clearly show forth the omnipotence and infinite knowledge of God, are most certain signs of a divine revelation, and are suited to the intelligence of all [can. 3 and 4].[58]

Each external proof is—to use an expression that appears later in the constitution—a "motive of credibility."[59] The statement above includes two motives, namely, miracles and prophecies, and a third is added later in the constitution: "The Church itself . . . is a very great and perpetual motive of credibility."[60] Rino Fisichella writes the following regarding motives of credibility:

> They are arguments that attest to the divine origin of revelation, arguments directed at reason. While analysis of the signs [of credibility] allows one to attain to the certainty of the revealed fact, it consequently allows one to conclude that the contents of revelation are worthy of belief.[61]

What Fisichella refers to as "the revealed fact" is more commonly referred to as the fact of revelation. Attainment of certainty about that fact is, importantly, distinguishable from but bound up with the contents of revelation deserving belief.

57. Dulles, *Assurance*, 228.
58. DB 1790; DS 3009. The alternate translation in brackets is from Tanner, *Decrees of Ecumenical Councils*, 2:807.
59. DB 1794; DS 3013.
60. DB 1794; DS 3013.
61. Fisichella, "Credibility," 195.

For further insight into the motives of credibility, it is useful to consider the slightly different wording employed in Schema III. It speaks of "miracles and prophecies, which when they reveal God's power and wisdom, are the most certain signs of divine speech."[62] This wording clarifies that the signs *establish* that what has been spoken is of divine origin. The word "proofs" in the constitution itself is not technical but strategic; it was selected for its capacity to firmly counter fideism and skepticism. Intelligence is marked by its ability to grasp that God has in fact spoken, and as a witness with perfect credibility, God's speech can be submitted to in a way that is "in accordance with reason." The phrase "which when" in the statement from Schema III above stipulates more vividly what the signs do to render nascent faith reasonable.

As extraordinary a gift it is to have available certain signs of divine speech, a conundrum immediately presents itself. On the one hand, "the signs of credibility . . . are not the formal motive of faith; they are . . . not its cause," as Juan Alfaro observes.[63] Yet, there is plainly *some* connection between one of the things the signs show forth, namely, the "infinite knowledge of God," and the formal motive of faith: the authority of God who reveals. The conundrum is how, in light of this, faith can remain a free response and a supernatural virtue.[64]

It is clarifying to discover that the framing of the motives, both in the constitution itself and in schemata, is informed by an already-mentioned encyclical: *Qui Pluribus*. A salient passage in this encyclical reads,

> Human reason . . . ought to search diligently for the fact of divine revelation so that it can know with certainty that God has spoken, and so render to Him . . . "a rational service" [Rom 12:1]. . . . Who does not know . . . that

---

62. Mansi, *Sacrorum Conciliorum*, 53:166. Latin: "Miracula et vaticinia, quae cum Dei potentiam et sapientiam revelant, divinae locutionis signa sunt certissima."

63. Alfaro, "Motive of Faith," 511. See also the canon related to this: DB 1814; DS 3035.

64. For the background of this problem, see Dulles, *Assurance*, 209.

nothing is more suitable to reason itself than to acquiesce and firmly adhere to those truths which it has been established were revealed by God, who can neither deceive nor be deceived?[65]

Awareness of God's omniscience before assenting makes that assenting suitable to reason but does not subtract from its status as free and supernatural. That status always holds, even in the case of a nonbeliever who directly witnesses a miracle.

More can be gathered about the status of the motives of credibility from the statement under consideration. God wills internal aids be joined by external proofs "in order that" the submission of faith is consonant with reason. That is, God wanted them to "be available" to human beings, as Schema III helps to clarify.[66]

Another choice by the fathers bolsters the point about availability and at the same time widens the range of the apologetic appeal of external proofs. Specifically, they "did not settle the question" of whether grace is required for external proofs to be "fully convincing," as Dulles observes.[67] If "the internal aids of the Holy Spirit" are involved, then grace is involved. However, for those concerned about an essential compromise of intellectual autonomy, the constitution leaves open the possibility of a fully convincing, natural grasp of the fact of revelation.[68]

Although the statement deems external proofs "suited to the intelligence of all," it remains the case that the supernatural virtue of faith is usually infused when one is an infant.[69] Moreover, unbaptized adults must overcome an array of biases and vices before

---

65. DB 1637; DS 2778.

66. Mansi, *Sacrorum Conciliorum*, 53:166. Latin: "Voluit Deus . . . praesto esse."

67. Dulles, *Assurance*, 211.

68. Dulles, *Assurance*, 212. Dulles adds that "'the interior instinct of God who invites [a person] to believe' . . . could . . . contribute to faith . . . , even though the believer might have no clear and distinct perception of grace as such" (216). Here Dulles quotes Aquinas, *Summa Theologica*, 2:1187, II-II, q. 2, a. 9, ad. 3.

69. As Ludwig Ott explains, "The faith which the infants lack is . . . replaced by the faith of the Church" (*Fundamentals of Catholic Dogma*, 359).

the assent of faith. In contemplating these points, it must be remembered that the constitution is written from the perspective of an institution seeking to be accountable.[70] The proofs are suited for all but not all must grasp them to satisfy such accountability.

A canon connected to the statement about faith being consonant with reason proscribes, in part, fideism. It reads,

> If anyone shall have said that miracles are not possible, and hence that all accounts of them, even those contained in Sacred Scripture, are to be banished among the fables and myths; or, that miracles can never be known with certitude, and that the divine origin of the Christian religion cannot be correctly proved by them: let him be anathema.[71]

The latter part of this canon, while certainly extending to skeptics of various types, also pertains to Roman Catholic theologians who reject miracles as effective motives of credibility—theologians such as Bautain.[72] For Bautain, the divine origin of the Christian religion is something one can be certain about in terms of adherence but not in terms of proof through the evidence of miracles. When the fathers "assert that the evident credibility of the Christian religion is demonstrable," writes Dulles, they are saying that "by using rational arguments it is possible to distinguish faith from gullibility and wishful thinking."[73]

In another relevant statement in chapter 3, the fathers continue to chart a course between fideism and rationalism. Their effort is aided by a quotation from the aforementioned Second Council of Orange:

> Although the assent of faith is by no means a blind movement of the intellect, nevertheless, no one can "assent to the preaching of the Gospel," as he must to attain salvation, "without the illumination and inspiration of the

---

70. For a reflection on this point, see Latourelle, "Apologetics II," 37–38.
71. DB 1813; DS 3034.
72. Horton, *Philosophy of Abbé Bautain*, 228.
73. Dulles, *Assurance*, 209–10.

Holy Spirit, who gives to all a sweetness in consenting to and believing in truth" ([Second] Council of Orange).[74]

On the first sentence, Dulles comments, "It seems to be implied that any individual must have access to sufficient evidence so that his or her faith is subjectively prudent."[75] Consulting Schema IV proves illuminating. There it is stated that faith is not "blind" and not "disconnected from the operation of the intellect" precisely because "we would not believe unless we saw that [revealed truth] is to be believed."[76] For his part, Smith contends that persons in possession of intelligence can arrive at a state in which there is "no *reasonable* doubt" regarding "the existence of God and the fact of revelation." What constitutes reasonable doubt varies from person to person. Smith provides an example: "[A] child who learns from his teacher, or from his catechism, that there is a God who has revealed certain truths has a *prudent conviction* regarding the preambles."[77]

A final relevant statement from chapter 3 moves from *fides qua creditur* (the faith by which [something] is believed) to *fides quae creditur* (the faith which is believed). It reads,

> By divine and Catholic faith, all those things must be believed which are contained in [the word of God as found in scripture and tradition], and those which are proposed by the Church, either in a solemn pronouncement

---

74. DB 1791; DS 3010. For the canon quoted in this passage, see DB 180; DS 377. It is worth noting the following verse from Hebrews, which is, surprisingly, not referred to in the statement or in the canon quoted: "Without faith it is impossible to please God, for whoever would approach him must believe that he exists and that he rewards those who seek him" (Heb 11:6).

75. Dulles, *Assurance*, 210.

76. Mansi, *Sacrorum Conciliorum*, 51:34. Latin: "Licet autem non crederemus, nisi videremus esse credendum, atque adeo fidei assensus nequaquam sit modus animi caecus, et ab intellectus operatione disiunctus." A footnote indicates that the beginning of this statement paraphrases Aquinas, *Summa Theologica*, 2:1172, II-II, q. 1, a. 4, ad. 2.

77. George Smith, "Faith and Revealed Truth," 15; emphasis added.

or in her ordinary and universal teaching power, to be believed as divinely revealed.[78]

The phrase "all those things must be believed," it should be noted, does not carry with it a requirement of rational inspection. "In saying 'I believe what the Church teaches,'" writes Dulles, "the Christian expresses a global assent that includes doctrines of which he or she as an individual might not be distinctly aware."[79]

3.4 Chapter 4 of the Constitution: Faith and Reason

The first salient statement in chapter 4 appears to be a restatement of a point already made in chapter 2. On closer inspection, it goes further:

> By enduring agreement the Catholic Church has held and holds that there is a twofold order of knowledge, distinct not only in principle but also in object: (1) in principle, indeed, because we know in one way by natural reason, in another by divine faith; (2) in object, however, because, in addition to things to which natural reason can attain, mysteries hidden in God are proposed to us for belief which, had they not been divinely revealed, could not become known [can. 1].[80]

---

78. DB 1792; DS 3011. The alternate translation in brackets is from Tanner, *Decrees of the Ecumenical Councils*, 2:807. The fathers here and elsewhere (DB 1787; DS 3006) stress that the word of God means the written word (Sacred Scripture) and the spoken word (Sacred Tradition).

79. Dulles, *Assurance*, 192. He goes on to clarify: "[Catholics] are not bound to accept, under pain of infidelity, *everything* taught by the magisterium. Most of the doctrines of the Church are taught noninfallibly and are . . . reformable. About these 'nondefinitive' teachings, the Catholic is entitled, for adequate reasons, to have doubts. Such doubts are not sins against the faith, but are held within faith" (234; emphasis added). Dulles's assessment should be read alongside the following caution found in ch. 3 of the constitution: "No one can . . . attain eternal life unless he or she perseveres in [faith] to the end" (Tanner, *Decrees of Ecumenical Councils*, 2:807). See DB 1793; DS 3012.

80. DB 1795; DS 3015.

What is new here is the invocation, for the first time in the constitution, of the term "mysteries." The mysteries the fathers have in mind are at least four: the Trinity, the Incarnation, the real presence of Christ in the sacraments, and the elevation of the human spirit through divine grace.[81]

Another key statement in chapter 4 provides further detail regarding the knowability of the mysteries of faith:

> Indeed, reason illustrated by faith, when it zealously, piously, and soberly seeks, attains with the help of God some understanding of the mysteries, and that a most profitable one, not only from the analogy of those things which it knows naturally, but also from the connection of the mysteries among themselves and with the last end of man; nevertheless, it is never capable of perceiving those mysteries in the way it does the truths which constitute its own proper object. For, divine mysteries by their nature exceed the created intellect so much that, even when handed down by revelation and accepted by faith, they nevertheless remain covered by the veil of faith itself, and wrapped in a certain mist, as it were, as long as in this mortal life, "we are absent from the Lord: for we walk by faith and not by sight" [2 Cor 5:6–7].[82]

Here the fathers once again navigate between fideism and rationalism. As Smith explains the nuance,

> A mystery is incomprehensible, . . . but it is not meaningless; it conveys a very definite meaning. The proposition that Jesus Christ is both God and man, that he is one person who has two natures, the human and the divine, is incomprehensible indeed; but it is not without meaning. It is full of meaning, so full that man with his finite mind will never exhaust it.[83]

---

81. Dulles, *Assurance*, 234. Latourelle remarks that "the principal mystery which God means to manifest is that of his salvific will, that is, the mystery of our participation in the divine life given by Christ" (*Theology of Revelation*, 265).

82. DB 1796; DS 3016.

83. George Smith, "Faith and Revealed Truth," 7–8.

Faith and Reason in Dei Filius

There are three ways, according to the statement, in which one can delve into such meaning.[84] Even so, the metaphor of mist is a caution on the limits of this venture; it is drawn from Pope Pius IX's *Gravissimas Inter*.[85] This 1862 letter was directed at Jakob Frohschammer (d. 1893), who, like Günther, exaggerated the capabilities of reason in relation to the mysteries of faith. Thomas Guarino sums up the position taken in the brief this way: "The created intellect (human or angelic) may achieve only a very limited cognitive penetration into the divine mysteries themselves."[86] When this topic reemerged at the council, one of the fathers requested for it to be clarified that "mysteries supersede our intellects in this life, but they do not surpass the intellects of the saints reigning in heaven."[87] The request was not granted.

Chapter 4 of the constitution goes on to provide its most explicit characterization of the relationship between faith and reason thus far:

> Although faith is above reason, nevertheless, between faith and reason no true dissension can ever exist, since the same God, who reveals mysteries and infuses faith, has bestowed on the human soul the light of reason; moreover, God cannot deny Himself, nor ever contradict truth with truth. But, a vain appearance of such a contradiction arises chiefly from this, that either the dogmas of faith have not been understood and interpreted according to the mind of the Church, or deceitful opinions are considered as the determinations of reason. Therefore, "every assertion contrary to the truth illuminated by faith, we define to be altogether false" [Lateran Council V, see n. 738].[88]

---

84. For a brief discussion of these three manners, see Wicks, *Doing Theology*, 18–19.

85. See DB 1673; DS 2856.

86. Guarino, "Vatican I," 72. The background of Guarino's remark is filled in by Ott: "God is for every created spirit, even in the state of supernatural elevation, incomprehensible.... The finite spirit can understand the infinite Essence of God in a finite manner only" (*Fundamentals of Catholic Dogma*, 23).

87. Guarino, "Vatican I," 77.

88. DB 1797; DS 3017.

To paraphrase this passage, a judgment made via the divinely bestowed light of reason cannot *truly* contradict an assent made via the divinely infused light of faith, for both types of light are from God. If the *appearance* of contradiction arises, either the former is the fruit of deceitful opinion or the latter is not in concord with "the mind of the Church."

As Denys Turner points out, applying the last sentence of the statement to the constitution itself yields a fact that is challenging to grasp: among those things which are contrary to the truth illuminated by faith is the claim that God cannot be known with certitude by the natural light of human reason from created things.[89] In other words, even if an atheistic philosopher came to *rationally* convince all Roman Catholics that one cannot know God in this way, they would still be required to *faithfully* affirm that one can.[90] This is the case for Roman Catholics because the possibility of natural knowledge of God has been "defined . . . by the College of Bishops gathered in council."[91]

A final salient statement from the constitution contains another explicit characterization of the relationship between faith and reason. It reads,

> Not only can faith and reason never be at variance with one another, but they also bring mutual help to each other, since right reasoning demonstrates the basis of faith and, illumined by its light, perfects the knowledge of divine things, while faith frees and protects reason from errors and provides it with manifold knowledge. Wherefore, the Church is so far from objecting to the culture of the human arts and sciences, that it aids and promotes this cultivation in many ways.[92]

---

89. Turner, *Faith, Reason*, 20.

90. Turner, *Faith, Reason*, 22.

91. Congregation for the Doctrine of the Faith, "Commentary on *Professio Fidei*," §5.

92. DB 1799; DS 3019. The way "demonstrates" is used here does not mark a contradiction with the selection of the milder "to know with certitude" in ch. 2 of the constitution. See Granderath, *Acta et Decreta*, 204.

Garrigou-Lagrange explains that by "the basis of faith," the fathers of the council mean the existence God, the authority of God who reveals (God can neither deceive nor be deceived), and the fact of revelation.[93] These three items are regularly referred to as "the preambles of faith" in theological manuals.[94] In the constitution, the first item was introduced in chapter 2; the second and third items were introduced in chapter 3. Here, in chapter 4, they are referred to collectively, and they are deemed to be the basis of faith. Importantly, they are the basis of faith "in the sense that they are a necessary prerequisite," not "in the sense of supplying the security of the edifice," as Smith observes.[95] It is not the case that a person who has made the act of faith has made an act any less certain if he or she has not demonstrated the preambles. However, it is also not the case that there would be no consequence to faith if reasoning overthrew the preambles. "If they were denied," writes Alfaro, "the falsehood of revealed doctrines would logically follow."[96]

---

93. Garrigou-Lagrange, *God*, 1:25.

94. Dulles, *History of Apologetics*, 120n82. The phrase itself is much older. It can be found in Aquinas, *Summa Theologica*, 1:12, I, q. 2, a. 2, ad. 1. For an overview of Aquinas's conception of the preambles, see Shanley, *Thomist Tradition*, 22–28.

95. George Smith, "Faith and Revealed Truth," 22. On the potential confusion building metaphors can cause when used in relation to the motives of credibility, see Knox, *Belief of Catholics*, 48.

96. Alfaro, "Preambles of Faith," 512–13.

4

Lonergan on Natural Knowledge of God

JUST AS CHAPTER 1 attended to just one dimension of the nineteenth-century debate about faith and reason, this chapter attends to just one twentieth-century interpretation of *Dei Filius*, the First Vatican Council's response to that debate. The interpretation is found in a paper on *Dei Filius* (hereafter, the constitution) delivered by Bernard Lonergan at the 1968 convention of the Catholic Theological Society of America. The paper, entitled "Natural Knowledge of God," unpacks what the constitution declares regarding what can be known about God through reason. This alone renders Lonergan worthy of consideration, but he also refers to the constitution in *Insight: A Study of Human Understanding*, published in 1957, and in *Method in Theology*, published in 1972. The first three sections of this chapter will review these texts, in chronological order.

What further renders Lonergan worthy of consideration is his relatedness to the philosophical backdrop of the constitution. Recall from chapter 1 of this book that Kleutgen, prior to serving as the main author of the constitution, attacked what McCool names "the post-Kantian epistemology of the intuitive *Vernunft*."[1]

---

1. McCool, *Nineteenth-Century Scholasticism*, 143.

Lonergan, surprisingly, engaged in something similar. As Michael Baur observes,

> Lonergan stresses throughout his writings [that] properly human knowing is never just a matter of "looking," that is, it is never just a matter of confronting or being affected by some content that is simply given to the knower (whether of a sensible or intelligible nature).[2]

Lonergan recounts that it was through the philosophy of Joseph Maréchal (d. 1944) that he "learnt to speak of human knowledge as not intuitive but discursive with the decisive component in judgment."[3]

That Lonergan's enterprise overlaps with one of Kleutgen's key concerns raises the question of the degree of overlap between their own epistemologies. A general sense of Lonergan's attitude toward Kleutgen's epistemology can be gathered from *Understanding and Being*, a corrected transcription of a seminar he gave at Saint Mary's University, Halifax, in 1958. In *Understanding and Being*, Lonergan twice refers to Georges Van Riet's (d. 1998) doctoral thesis, "L' épistémologie thomiste: Recherches sur le problème de la connaissance dans l'école thomiste contemporaine," published in English as *Thomistic Epistemology: Studies Concerning the Problem of Cognition in the Contemporary Thomistic School*. As part of his first reference, Lonergan sums up a typology that Van Riet offers for grouping Thomistic stances on epistemology. Lonergan writes,

> Van Riet divides the [Thomistic] philosophers into classes. First, there are those whose epistemology is fundamentally a matter of confrontation; and there are subdivisions under this heading. Secondly, there are those who hold an epistemology that is based upon understanding, comprehension, intelligence; and there are subdivisions here too. Finally, he has a category of epistemologies that are based upon judgment, and he

---

2. Baur, "Kant, Lonergan, and Fichte," 95. See Lonergan, *Understanding and Being*, 159; *Method in Theology*, 238.

3. Lonergan, "*Insight*: Revisited," 265. For the background and a critique of Maréchal's project, see Bradley, "Transcendental Critique."

divides them into two main classes: those that depend upon general judgments, and those that depend upon the act of judgment itself.[4]

After lining up Lonergan's summary of Van Riet's typology and the typology itself, one can infer Lonergan's view of Kleutgen based on where Van Riet's places him, namely, in the first part of the third group.[5] Because the present book does not seek to expound on or defend Lonergan's epistemology, let it simply be said that Lonergan does not belong to the same group as Kleutgen.[6] For the project of reassessment, this is all that matters. When, in chapter 5, Lonergan's own characterization of faith and reason is explored, it need only be remembered that his characterization flows out of an epistemology distinct from Kleutgen's. At the same time, Lonergan is sympathetic to a philosophical tension extant between the lines of the constitution. This renders him an independent but not disconnected figure in the debate about faith and reason that the constitution marks a response to.

This chapter will conclude with an evaluation of Lonergan's interpretation of the constitution. The evaluation will consider two different criticisms. Section 4 will examine a direct criticism advanced by Alan Vincelette. Section 5 will examine an indirect criticism found in the writing of Steven A. Long.

---

4. Lonergan, *Understanding and Being*, 103.

5. Van Riet gives examples of thinkers for each group, which would appear to fit into Lonergan's account of the taxonomy as follows. In the first group: Father Gény, Msgr. Farges, Father de Tonquédec, Gilson, Count Domet de Vorges, Msgr. Noël, Father de Vries, Father Brunner, Father Picard, Msgr. Zamboni. In the second group: Balmès, Peillaube, Lepidi, Gardeil, Garrigou-Lagrange, Roland-Gosselin, Maritain, Jolivet, Verneaux. In the first part of the third group: Kleutgen, Rickaby, Mercier, Sentroul, Boyer, Romeyer. In the second part of the third group: Maréchal, Rousselot, Rabeau. See Van Riet, *Thomistic Epistemology*, 2:289–90. For a more recently composed typology, see "Hallmarks and Species of Thomism," ch. 2, in Rowland, *Catholic Theology*.

6. Readers interested in why this is the case may consult McCool, *Nineteenth-Century Scholasticism*, 261–67.

4.1 Natural Knowledge of God in *Insight*

Insight was written from 1949 to 1953, revised at the publisher's request from 1954 to 1955, and published in 1957. The location of the book's treatment of natural knowledge of God is its nineteenth chapter, entitled "General Transcendent Knowledge." Confirmation of this comes by way of the book's epilogue. There Lonergan writes, "The Catholic thinker . . . must . . . acknowledge that by the natural light of human reason man can know with certitude the existence of God."[7] The paraphrasing and endorsement of the constitution are unmistakable in this statement. And in the very next paragraph, Lonergan writes,

> Our first eighteen chapters were written solely in the light of human intelligence and reasonableness and without any presupposition of God's existence, without any appeal to the authority of the church, and without any explicit deference to the genius of St Thomas Aquinas.[8]

The phraseology here places chapter 19 of *Insight* under the umbrella of natural knowledge of God. Even though Lonergan makes no reference to the constitution in the chapter, his claims are made against the backdrop of what the "Catholic thinker . . . must . . . acknowledge."

At the outset of chapter 19, Lonergan identifies strictly ocular models of knowing as an obstacle to arriving at general transcendent knowledge. He writes, "A first step towards transcendence . . . is to reject the mistaken supposition that knowing consists in taking a look."[9] It cannot be accidental, then, that when Lonergan mentions in passing that "positivists and Kantians . . . are loud in their negations of the possibility of transcendent knowledge," he happens to name two groups who embrace the mistaken

---

7. Lonergan, *Insight*, 765. He makes two explicit references to the constitution elsewhere in *Insight* (756, 761), but these pertain to the mysteries of faith and to revelation, not natural knowledge of God.

8. Lonergan, *Insight*, 765; abbreviation "St" in the original; word "church" is lowercase in the original.

9. Lonergan, *Insight*, 658.

supposition.[10] Although he only intermittently refers to these groups in the course of chapter 19, their "negations" are most certainly in the back of his mind as he writes. Lonergan thus tailors his argument for the attainability of general transcendent knowledge in a way that meets the criticisms of positivists and Kantians. This becomes a more dominant concern eleven years later in "Natural Knowledge of God," which will be examined shortly.

Lonergan summarily describes the manner in which one can acquire general transcendent knowledge. He writes,

> Knowledge of transcendent being involves both intelligent grasp and reasonable affirmation. But before we can affirm reasonably, we must grasp intelligently; and before we can grasp transcendent being intelligently, we have to extrapolate from proportionate being.[11]

In stating that knowledge of transcendent being involves more than one cognitional operation, and later that "the existence of God . . . is known as the conclusion to an argument,"[12] Lonergan firmly moves away from intuitionist accounts of such knowledge and upholds a discursive approach.

Lonergan begins his fuller account of the acquisition of general transcendent knowledge by considering a question: "What . . . is being?"[13] He then sketches several human vantage points from which one can pose the question but finds each of them unable to arrive at an answer. Lonergan writes, "The pure notion of being raises all questions but answers none. The heuristic notion envisages all answers but determines none. Particular inquiries solve some questions but not all." Such dead ends, so to speak, ultimately lead him to posit "an unrestricted act of understanding,"

---

10. Lonergan, *Insight*, 664. In the epilogue, Lonergan laments that "we live in the midst of a sensate culture, in which very many men, insofar as they acknowledge any hegemony of truth, give their allegiance not to a divine revelation, nor to a theology, nor to a philosophy, nor even to an intellectualist science, but to science interpreted in a positivistic and pragmatic fashion" (766).

11. Lonergan, *Insight*, 664.

12. Lonergan, *Insight*, 695.

13. Lonergan, *Insight*, 665.

the content of which is "the idea of being."[14] Earlier in *Insight*, Lonergan deemed the *notion* of being "the all-inclusive heuristic anticipation issuing from an unrestricted desire to know."[15] This all-inclusive heuristic anticipation is captured in the question, What is being? One cannot answer the question, but one knows the kind of act that is necessary to answer it and what the content of that act would be: the idea of being. On this basis, Lonergan writes, "We have extrapolated from the question, What is being? to the absolutely transcendent idea of being."[16]

The idea of being—if it exists—marks the achievement of what the notion of being can at best strive for: understanding everything about everything. Yet the impossibility of an unrestricted act of understanding or something akin to it in the human mind does not cut one off from further inquiry into the matter as Kant and Hegel maintain.[17] Lonergan writes, "While man cannot enjoy an unrestricted act of understanding and so answer the question, What is being? still he can determine a number of features of the answer."[18]

Lonergan goes on to treat a number of technical issues revolving around causality.[19] Bracketing these issues, it can simply be noted that he ultimately identifies the idea of being with God.[20]

14. Lonergan, *Insight*, 666.

15. Lonergan, *Insight*, 447.

16. Lonergan, *Insight*, 666. As Patrick Byrne explains, "The extrapolation by way of analogy enabled Lonergan to speak meaningfully about the unrestricted act of understanding without actually knowing its content (i.e., without actually understanding in an unrestricted fashion)" ("God and the Statistical Universe," 358).

17. As Michael Vertin explains, Kant holds that "we lack the intellectual intuition that would yield speculative knowledge of things in themselves," and Hegel holds that "we lack the exhaustive understanding that would display the intelligible relations between any given thing and everything else in the universe" ("Properly Situating Philosophical Arguments," 3).

18. Lonergan, *Insight*, 667.

19. For analysis, see St. Amour, "Validity of Extrinsic Causality."

20. Lonergan, *Insight*, 680. Instead of emphasizing the absurdity of an infinite regress of causes, Lonergan emphasizes the absurdity of an infinite regress of restricted acts of understanding.

This establishes God as something conceivable within human consciousness but nothing more. The point is an important one, for Lonergan's approach, moving forward, will be to treat "the notion of God" before addressing "whether this notion refers to existent reality."[21] Lonergan warns that divergence from what he names the "basic position"[22] and the retention of any "bias"[23] yields "misconceived and confused" perspectives on the issue.[24] This marks an early sense of the need for some type of intellectual conversion on the part of the knower before he or she can understand and affirm an argument for the existence of God.

Using only the notion of God, Lonergan enumerates a set of divine attributes: the primary intelligible, the primary truth, the primary being, without any defect, the primary good, perfect loving, self-explanatory, unconditioned, necessary, one, simple, timeless, eternal, omnipotent, omniscient, free, without change, creator, conserver, first agent, final cause, and personal.[25] Many of these attributes are listed in chapter 1 of the constitution—specifically, and in the terminology used there: one, true, Creator, omnipotent, eternal, infinite in every perfection, one, simple, and unchangeable.[26] Recall, however, that the constitution does not declare it a part of faith—even if it is the case—that these and the other attributes listed can be grasped by reason. Thus, when

21. Lonergan, *Insight*, 680–81.

22. "It will be a basic position (1) if the real is the concrete universe of being and not a subdivision of the 'already out there now'; (2) if the subject becomes known when it affirms itself intelligently and reasonably and so is not known yet in any prior 'existential' state; and (3) if objectivity is conceived as a consequence of intelligent inquiry and critical reflection, and not as a property of vital anticipation, extroversion, and satisfaction. On the other hand, it will be a basic counterposition if it contradicts one or more of the basic positions" (Lonergan, *Insight*, 413; indentation removed).

23. Lonergan, *Insight*, 704.

24. Lonergan, *Insight*, 707.

25. Lonergan, *Insight*, 681–92. As Ulf Jonsson observes, the first six attributes are derived from the concept of an unrestricted act of understanding; the remainder are derived from the third attribute (*Foundations for Knowing God*, 157).

26. DB 1782; DS 3001.

Lonergan grasps them "solely in the light of human intelligence and reasonableness," he is expressing a personal achievement, not adherence to the constitution.

What remains to be detailed is the means by which Lonergan—and potentially any reader of *Insight*—affirms the existence of God. Lonergan moves from treating God as an object of thought to treating God as an object of affirmation by way of an argument: "If the real is completely intelligible, God exists. But the real is completely intelligible. Therefore, God exists."[27] I will refrain from elaborating on the argument itself; works doing this are available.[28] What is important is the argument's character, which is captured in this statement from the epilogue: "Our first eighteen chapters were followed by a nineteenth and twentieth that revealed the inevitability with which the affirmation of God and the search of intellect for faith arise out of a sincere acceptance of scientific presuppositions and precepts."[29] Here Lonergan describes the affirmation of God as arising out of an acceptance of scientific presuppositions and precepts—items that, to reiterate, he grasps "solely in the light of human intelligence and reasonableness."

Having affirmed the existence of God, Lonergan goes on to reject ontological arguments, including those that Anselm and Descartes advance.[30] A question arises here regarding Lonergan's appraisal of arguments that proceed more—or at least, more explicitly—on the side of the object. One wonders, for instance, how he would see his argument in relation to Aquinas's Five Ways.

As it happens, Lonergan addresses the Five Ways in chapter 19 of *Insight*. In one instance, he writes, "[The Five Ways] in which Aquinas proves the existence of God are so many particular cases

27. Lonergan, *Insight*, 695. For a contemporary development of Lonergan's argument, see "A Lonerganian Proof for God's Existence," ch. 4, in Spitzer, *New Proofs*.

28. For an overview of the argument, see Tyrrell, *Lonergan's Philosophy of God*. For a brief summary of early criticisms of the argument, namely by James Albertson, Ronald Hepburn, J. P. Mackey, and David Burrell, see Braxton, "Knowledge of God," 330–32.

29. Lonergan, *Insight*, 765.

30. Lonergan, *Insight*, 693.

of the general statement that the proportionate universe is incompletely intelligible and that complete intelligibility is demanded."[31] Alicia Jaramillo points out that this focus on the demand for complete intelligibility does not mark an abandonment of long-standing cosmological arguments.[32]

4.2 Natural Knowledge of God in "Natural Knowledge of God"

Lonergan begins his 1968 convention paper, "Natural Knowledge of God," as follows: "By natural knowledge of God I shall understand the knowledge of God intended by the dogmatic constitution *Dei Filius* of [the First Vatican Council]."[33] He then reproduces, in Latin, the core of the statement on natural knowledge of God. In English, the core of the statement reads, "God, the beginning and end of all things, can be known with certitude by the natural light of human reason from created things."[34] Following this, he reproduces, again in Latin, the entire canon pertaining to the statement. In English, the canon reads,

> If anyone shall have said that the one true God, our Creator and our Lord, cannot be known with certitude by those things which have been made, by the natural light of human reason: let him be anathema.[35]

Lonergan states that his interpretation of these parts of the constitution is "based on . . . Pottmeyer's study of the history of *Dei Filius*."[36] Central to Lonergan's interpretation is his belief that the

---

31. Lonergan, *Insight*, 700.
32. Jaramillo, "Raising Question of God," 248.
33. Lonergan, "Natural Knowledge of God," 117.
34. DB 1785; DS 3004.
35. DB 1806; DS 3026.
36. Lonergan, "Natural Knowledge of God," 117. The study referred to in the 1968 publication of the paper is Pottmeyer, "Höhepunkt der Auseinandersetzung," 3:164–76. The study referred to in the 1996 publication of the paper is Pottmeyer, *Glaube*, 168–204.

constitution deals only with the possibility of natural knowledge of God. He writes, "Vatican I was not speaking of a *quaestio facti* but of a *quaestio iuris*, not of conditions of actuality but of conditions of possibility."[37] For Lonergan, evidence of this is found in what Pottmeyer refers to as Schema III. Present there, Lonergan observes, are two specifications regarding natural knowledge of God. In translation, the first is that "fallen man" can acquire natural knowledge of God; the second is that "it is not wholly necessary that this doctrine regarding God be handed down." Lonergan judges that the *absence* of these specifications from Schema IV onward show that what the fathers of the council treat is a question of law, not a question of fact.[38]

Lonergan goes on to register that "the knowledge in question is not immediate but mediated, and it is mediated . . . by creatures."[39] Note that the "is" here should be taken in the light of the two absences above. For Lonergan, the constitution "does not commit itself either to saying that the possibility [of the light of reason reaching certain knowledge of God] ever was realized or to predicting that it ever would be realized."[40]

In the remainder of the text, Lonergan surveys and responds to seven "difficulties perhaps commonly felt about the doctrine of natural knowledge of God."[41] It is important to note that the doctrine Lonergan refers to here is specifically that which is set out in the constitution. Lonergan surveys difficulties, or better, objections, from both intra-ecclesial and extra-ecclesial perspectives. In what follows, two of the objections that Lonergan surveys and responds to are examined.

A first objection is that many contemporary senses of the word "object" preclude God from being an object. God cannot be an object in the Kantian sense, asserts Lonergan, because for

---

37. Lonergan, "Natural Knowledge of God," 133. Lonergan appears to be drawing from Pottmeyer, *Glaube*, 195.

38. Lonergan, "Natural Knowledge of God," 118.

39. Lonergan, "Natural Knowledge of God," 118.

40. Lonergan, "Natural Knowledge of God," 119.

41. Lonergan, "Natural Knowledge of God," 121.

Kant "our cognitional activity is restricted to a world of possible experience and that [is] a world not of metaphysical realities but of sensible phenomena." Nor can God be an object within "atomism, positivism, or empiricism, for the only discourse considered meaningful is discourse that can be reduced to, or be verified in, or at least be falsifiable by sensible objects."[42] Further still, God cannot be an object in the sense modern science has given the term. Modern science verifies hypotheses by returning to data, and "God is not among the data of sense" or "the data of human consciousness."[43]

Lonergan responds that God *can* be an object if object is taken in the sense that accords with his philosophy: "An object is what is intended in questioning and becomes known by answering questions."[44] Lonergan admits that this approach does not dispense with the need for verification. He writes, "It [the need for verification] is a need disclosed to us by what Vatican I referred to as the natural light of human reason, by what I should name our power to ask and answer questions."[45] Here attention is turned to the source of the need for verification: the human mind itself. He continues, "This principle, the human mind itself, does not need verification for its validation."[46] The human mind, then, is "the unverifiable principle by which we proceed from knowledge of this world to knowledge of God."[47] Lonergan then elucidates how we proceed in this way:

> If human knowing consists in asking and answering questions, if ever further questions arise, if the further questions are given honest answers then, as I have argued elsewhere at some length, we can and do arrive at knowledge of God.[48]

---

42. Lonergan, "Natural Knowledge of God," 122.
43. Lonergan, "Natural Knowledge of God," 120.
44. Lonergan, "Natural Knowledge of God," 121.
45. Lonergan, "Natural Knowledge of God," 125.
46. Lonergan, "Natural Knowledge of God," 126.
47. Lonergan, "Natural Knowledge of God," 124.
48. Lonergan, "Natural Knowledge of God," 127. Lonergan also comments

As a footnote in the text indicates, the "elsewhere" he is referring to is chapter 19 of *Insight*, which was reviewed above.

A second objection to the constitution's declaration on natural knowledge of God is that such knowledge "is not attained without moral judgments and existential decisions," and that these acts "do not occur without God's grace."[49] Lonergan's response is that this objection is not applicable to the constitution, given the intent of the fathers of the council. He writes,

> One misinterprets Vatican I if one fancies it is speaking, not about a *quaestio iuris*, but about a *quaestio facti*. The *quaestio iuris* is (1) whether there exists a valid argument for God's existence and (2) whether the apprehension of that argument is an *actus supernaturalis quoad substantiam*. Natural knowledge of God is denied if one holds that there is no valid argument or if one holds that apprehending the argument is an intrinsically supernatural act. Natural knowledge of God is affirmed if one holds that there is a valid argument and if one holds that apprehending the argument is intrinsically natural.[50]

That the early Lonergan falls into the latter category—those who affirm natural knowledge of God—is clear from chapter 19 of *Insight*, where Lonergan supplies an argument for God's existence "solely in the light of human intelligence and reasonableness." One wonders, though, where Lonergan now stands on the *quaestio facti*.

Lonergan holds that the *quaestio facti* concerns the "conditions of someone actually grasping a valid argument for

---

that in the constitution natural knowledge of God "is not immediate but mediated, and it is mediated not by revelation but by creation" (118).

49. Lonergan, "Natural Knowledge of God," 133.

50. Lonergan, "Natural Knowledge of God," 133. It is worth registering here an opinion put forth decades before Lonergan delivered "Natural Knowledge of God." According to Marcel Chossat, to say that "*in fact*, without supernatural aid, man does not arrive at the knowledge of God" is compatible with the constitution, but to say that "*in law*, without supernatural aid, man does not arrive at the true knowledge of God" is incompatible with the constitution ("Dieu [Connaissance naturelle de]," 4.1:864; emphasis in original).

God's existence."[51] Since the range of conditions is so wide, from one's physical health to one's sinful habits, he sees a complete treatment of the *quaestio facti* as nearly impossible. Nevertheless, the *quaestio facti* is of import, and Lonergan's stance on the matter exhibits sympathy with the objection that he is responding to. He writes, "I do not think that in this life people arrive at natural knowledge of God without God's grace, but what I do not doubt is that the knowledge they so attain is natural."[52] In writing this, Lonergan upholds his commitment to the view that apprehending an argument for God is not an intrinsically supernatural act. Ulf Jonsson offers the following reflection on Lonergan's remark:

> A consistent striving to perform one's cognitive operations . . . in a reasonable way is the fruit of a moral decision, and one's moral striving is itself but an element in a more comprehensive human self-transcendence towards the gift of God's grace.[53]

Amid the same reflection, Jonsson writes,

> Although it is the case that a reasonable judgment on the validity of an argument for knowledge of God is apprehended by the natural light of reason, such a judgment *de facto* presupposes that the judging human subject has made moral decisions sustained by supernatural grace.[54]

The wider context of judgment that Jonsson elucidates here is something that, according to Lonergan, the fathers of the council did not pronounce on.

---

51. Lonergan, "Natural Knowledge of God," 133. He elaborates: "An adequate account would include every entity that conditioned the actual occurrence."

52. Lonergan, "Natural Knowledge of God," 133.

53. Jonsson, *Foundations for Knowing God*, 190.

54. Jonsson, *Foundations for Knowing God*, 190. For additional reflection, see "Religious Experience, Reflection, and Philosophy of God," ch. 3, in Kanaris, *Bernard Lonergan's Philosophy*.

4.3 Natural Knowledge of God in *Method in Theology*

Lonergan's treatment of natural knowledge of God in *Method in Theology*, published in 1972, mainly unfolds in the sections entitled "The Question of God" and "The Function of Systematics."

The section "The Question of God" rests in "Religion," chapter 4 of *Method in Theology*. In this section, Lonergan seeks only to defend this claim: "The question of God . . . lies within man's horizon."[55] Consequently, his approach resembles the first half of the chapter "General Transcendent Knowledge" in *Insight* and the first half of "Natural Knowledge of God"—the halves where Lonergan is defending the viability of the God-question, not supplying an answer to it. Explicating the emergence of the question, he writes,

> It [the question of God] is not a matter of image or feeling, of concept or judgment. They pertain to answers. It is a question. It rises out of our conscious intentionality, out of the *a priori* structured drive that promotes us from experiencing to the effort to understand, from understanding to the effort to judge truly, from judging to the effort to choose rightly. In the measure that we advert to our own questioning and proceed to question it, there arises the question of God.[56]

There is an acknowledgment by Lonergan that the question of God manifests itself differently depending on the historical and cultural setting. Nevertheless, he finds the question itself to lie beneath the differences:

> However much religious or irreligious answers differ, however much there differ the questions they explicitly raise, still at their root there is the same transcendental tendency of the human spirit that questions, that questions without restriction, that questions the significance

---

55. Lonergan, *Method in Theology*, 103.
56. Lonergan, *Method in Theology*, 103.

of its own questioning, and so comes to the question of God.[57]

Notably, the question of God arises not just from one's tendency to question without restriction but also thinking about the significance of that tendency.

Attention can now turn to the section "The Function of Systematics,"[58] which appears in "Systematics," chapter 13 of *Method in Theology*. Lonergan paraphrases the constitution's assertion that "reason illustrated by faith" can attain "some understanding" of the mysteries of faith.[59] He then writes, "Out of the Augustinian, Anselmian, Thomist tradition, despite an intervening heavy overlay of conceptualism, [the First Vatican Council] retrieved the notion of understanding."[60] This marks the only appearance of the word "conceptualism" in *Method in Theology*, and its usage is one of exoneration. That Lonergan *does not* find conceptualism to be operative in one of the constitution's key statements introduces the possibility that he might not find it operative elsewhere in the document. Now, it is important to note that while Lonergan's statement above pertains to the circulation of conceptualism before the council, he also found it to be prevalent after the council. During a 1958 question and answer session, Lonergan remarked,

> If you look up the type of Latin scholastic manual that was still current between 1926 and 1929, when I was studying philosophy, you'll find an account of intellect that doesn't at any stage have anything to say about understanding anything. You form concepts, and they're little nuggets. And they're functions of the thing; they're not dependent upon any intelligently conscious process; they're first; the first element of intellectual knowledge

---

57. Lonergan, *Method in Theology*, 103. For Lonergan's clearest outline of the four forms of the question of God, see Lonergan, "Philosophy of God," 206–7.

58. Lonergan, *Method in Theology*, 335–40.

59. DB 1796; DS 3016.

60. Lonergan, *Method in Theology*, 336.

is the concept. Then you compare concepts, and they're either contradictory, or necessarily related, or neither the one nor the other. Then you make judgments, and you make judgments in virtue of the sufficiency of the evidence. And what's the evidence? Well, it's your concept.[61]

The likelihood of Lonergan finding conceptualism inoperative in other parts of the constitution is lowered when one considers the implications of his own commitment to move away from it. These implications are brought to light in an outline of conceptualism put forth by John McDermott:

> For conceptualist Thomists, being, i.e., all of reality, is grasped in an analogous concept that tends to be interpreted along the model of an abstract concept of an essence. Truth consists primarily in the con-*form*-ity of the mind with reality that occurs in the passive intellect. Concepts so formed naturally encourage a static perspective on reality and support clear distinctions: between intellect and will, matter and form, body and soul, concept and judgment, world and God, natural and supernatural, reason and faith, etc.[62]

One can reasonably anticipate in Lonergan's writings, then, a softer or more nuanced distinction between reason and faith, as well as between the natural and supernatural. The question immediately arises, of course, as to how Lonergan will engage with some statements in the constitution, such as: "There is a twofold order of knowledge, distinct . . . in principle . . . because we know in one way by natural reason, in another by divine faith."[63] Some of this engagement materializes in what follows, but the bulk of engagement will be seen in chapter 5 of this book.

---

61. Lonergan, *Understanding and Being*, 350. Lonergan operated within and at the culmination of what McCool describes as a shift from "closed conceptualism" to "open intellectualism" in Thomism (McCool, *Nineteenth-Century Scholasticism*, 242).

62. McDermott, "Faith, Reason, and Freedom," 318; emphasis in original.

63. DB 1795; DS 3015.

Lonergan's explicit discussion of the constitution's statement on natural knowledge of God occurs within his argument for "an integration of natural with systematic theology."[64] A necessary condition of this integration is the abandonment of the view that objectivity results from escaping subjectivity. In accord with his emphasis on the *quaestio facti* in "Natural Knowledge of God," Lonergan here calls for a consideration of the subject not in the abstract but in the concrete, where objectivity is bound up with intellectual, moral, and religious conversion.[65] Since these conversions are integral to the argument Lonergan is making, it is worth reproducing his basic description of them in full:

> Intellectual conversion is ... the elimination of ... [t]he myth ... that knowing is like looking, that objectivity is seeing what is there to be seen and not seeing what is not there, and that the real is what is out there now to be looked at.... Moral conversion changes the criterion of one's decisions and choices from satisfactions to values.... Religious conversion is being grasped by ultimate concern. It is other-worldly falling in love. It is total and permanent self-surrender without conditions, qualifications, reservations. But it is such a surrender, not as an act, but as a dynamic state that is prior to and principle of subsequent acts.[66]

Lonergan goes on to address the constitution directly, and his comments revolve around conflict that some might perceive between his emphasis on conversion and the document's statement on natural knowledge of God. He writes,

> It may be objected ... that this transition from the abstract to the concrete, from proof to conversion, does not square with the claim of [the First Vatican Council] that

---

64. Lonergan, *Method in Theology*, 339. Even before the publication of *Method in Theology*, Lonergan remarked, "I'd be quite ready to say: let's drop chapter XIX out of *Insight* and put it inside of theology" ("Interview," 224).

65. Lonergan, *Method in Theology*, 338.

66. Lonergan, *Method in Theology*, 238–40.

through creatures God can be known with certainty by the natural light of human reason (DS 3004, 3026).[67]

The response to this objection provided by Lonergan involves a reiteration of his contention, already seen in "Natural Knowledge of God," that the constitution treats only the *quaestio iuris*. About the statement on natural knowledge of God, he writes,

> [It] tacitly prescinds from the actual order in which we live. The third schema of *Dei Filius*, drawn up by Fr. Joseph Kleutgen, read in the canon: "per ea quae facta sunt, naturali ratione ab homine lapso certo cognosci et demonstrari posse." The final version, however, makes no mention of fallen man and, in view of the abstract classicism then prevalent, is perhaps most simply understood to refer to the state of pure nature.[68]

Charles Hefling points out that "subjectivity and meaning can safely be omitted . . . on the classicist assumption that human nature is pretty much the same always and everywhere."[69] If it is true that this kind of thinking permeates the statement on natural knowledge of God, then Lonergan's "transition from the abstract to the concrete" is a wider angle on—rather than a cut away from—that statement.

It is worth mentioning the footnote that Lonergan affixes to the phrase "pure nature" at the end of the statement above. In this footnote, he refers to three texts, the first being his own "Natural Knowledge of God" as a whole. The third text referred to is Pottmeyer's *Der Glaube vor dem Anspruch der Wissenschaft*, and Lonergan specifies the same page range that he did at the outset of

---

67. Lonergan, *Method in Theology*, 338; DS numbers in the original.

68. Lonergan, *Method in Theology*, 338; Lonergan's ellipses at beginning and end of Latin quotation have been removed. It is worth acknowledging that Lonergan is certainly not the only one to hold this view. McCool, for example, holds it as well: "The baroque scholastic theology of the state of 'pure nature' . . . affected the wording of *Dei Filius* and . . . was not concerned with the historical order in which concrete man actually encountered the personal God of creation and revelation" (*Nineteenth-Century Scholasticism*, 221).

69. Hefling, "Philosophy, Theology, and God," 121.

"Natural Knowledge of God."[70] There is significant continuity, then, between "Natural Knowledge of God" and *Method in Theology*. At the same time, there is novelty. The second text referred to in the footnote is an article by David Coffey entitled "Natural Knowledge of God: Reflections on Romans 1:18–32." Restricted to a footnote, and referred to as a whole, precisely how much of the article serves as a basis for Lonergan's thought on the topic is unclear. Nonetheless, it is worth summarizing the article's salient points.

Coffey rejects the "exegesis of the pericope of Rom 1" adopted by the fathers, but he does not believe this renders him "condemned by the Council" since, on the one hand, "the reference to Rom 1 is nothing more than an illustration of the doctrine, and hence does not enjoy magisterial authority," and on the other, he upholds the constitution's "doctrine of the possibility of natural knowledge of God."[71] As for his own exegesis of the pericope of Rom 1, Coffey writes,

> [Paul] was speaking of the distant past, when [the gentiles] knew [God] as Adam did, before they committed the sin that led them into their present condition of ignorance. He does not say there that they ever knew Him from reason alone, but rather that when they knew Him by faith they knew Him by reason too, from His creation, and when by idolatry they lost their faith this creation remained as a permanent witness to the God against whom they sinned and were sinning.[72]

Coffey goes on to consider a situation where God purportedly *is* known from reason alone. "The First Mover," contends Coffey, "is not the Creator, He has no providence or plan for the world, He is completely self-centered, He is unloving and unloved." At the same time, "He is said, e.g., to be pure act, to be immaterial and intelligent."[73] The question arises as to whether these latter attributes suffice to identify the First Mover with God. Coffey writes,

---

70. Namely, Pottmeyer, *Glaube*, 168–204.
71. Coffey, "Natural Knowledge of God," 690–91.
72. Coffey, "Natural Knowledge of God," 682.
73. Coffey, "Natural Knowledge of God," 684.

> The simple answer "No" must be given, for the false statements have the effect of falsifying the total conception of God. Theoretically, Aristotle could have achieved a totally (by the standard of natural theology) true understanding of God; yet, because of his human weakness, he fell short of this, with the result that the understanding he did achieve was falsified. If this was the best that the wisest of the Greeks could achieve, what more could be expected of lesser men?[74]

Coffey goes on to explain how he can hold, without breaking away from the constitution, that the god known by Aristotle is not the true God:

> These remarks are not in opposition to the affirmation of man's physical power to know God both adequately (to the extent that His nature is knowable through the universe) and accurately. What is asserted here is the moral necessity that man apart from revelation will falsify his natural knowledge of God.[75]

In the final sentence of this quotation, there is an echo of Lonergan's view that moral conversion can play a role in the attainment of natural knowledge of God. Lonergan does not follow Coffey, however, in holding that such knowledge is inevitably falsified in the absence of moral (or religious) conversion.[76] Although it is "by way of exception," Lonergan, in *Method in Theology*, holds that "certain knowledge of God's existence" can "precede the acceptance of God's gift of his love."[77] More will be said about this statement in chapter 5 of this book, where the spotlight shifts from Lonergan's interpretation of the constitution to his personal stance on acts that lead to faith.

---

74. Coffey, "Natural Knowledge of God," 685.
75. Coffey, "Natural Knowledge of God," 685.
76. Lonergan, *Method in Theology*, 267–68.
77. Lonergan, *Method in Theology*, 339.

4.4 First Evaluation of Lonergan's Interpretation of the Constitution

To evaluate Lonergan's interpretation of the constitution is to evaluate "Natural Knowledge of God," the most direct treatment found in his corpus, as well as *Method in Theology*, which is less direct but the more mature of the two.[78] As stated at the outset of this chapter, the evaluation will involve a consideration of two criticisms. The first of these is put forth by Vincelette.

Vincelette criticizes the significance Lonergan affords, in "Natural Knowledge of God" and *Method in Theology*, to the removal of "fallen man" from a canon.[79] To reiterate, Schema III reads, "known with certitude . . . by fallen man,"[80] whereas the constitution simply reads, "known with certitude."[81] Vincelette highlights the deputation on faith's response to a request for chapter 2 of the constitution to read, "God can be known by the light of natural reason, as it is now."[82] The deputation declined "since the things which are taught in this doctrine are generally to be regarded as true, whether man be taken in a state of pure nature, or in a state of fallen nature."[83] The point is remade when it is said that

---

78. Lonergan, "Doctrinal Pluralism," 88–93, also treats the constitution but is essentially a summary of it.

79. The criticism occurs in a footnote: Vincelette, *Recent Catholic Philosophy*, 263n40. Vincelette provides translations of Latin material he refers to, but personal and Deferrari translations will be given here to maintain consistency with other chapters of this book.

80. Mansi, *Sacrorum Conciliorum*, 53:168. Latin: "Ab homine lapso certo cognosci."

81. DB 1806; DS 3026.

82. Vacant, *Études théologiques*, 1:658. Latin: "Deum naturali rationis lumine, uti nunc est, posse cognosci." Vincelette provides English translations of quotations from Vacant, but personal translations of those quotations are given here for consistency.

83. Vacant, *Études théologiques*, 1:658. Latin: "Cum ea quae in ista doctrina docentur, generatim vera habendi sint, sive sumatur homo in statu naturae purae, sive in statu naturae lapsae."

the statement on natural knowledge of God is "about the condition of human nature in general."[84]

Lonergan's phraseology in *Method in Theology*, his mature work on the matter, only partially evades Vincelette's criticism. Recall that Lonergan saw the statement on natural knowledge of God as "perhaps" referring to the state of pure nature. The evidence above supports Lonergan. And recall Lonergan's view that the statement "prescinds from"—that is, withdraws *attention* from—"the actual order in which we live." Once again, the evidence supports Lonergan. What weakens Lonergan's interpretation of the constitution is the gravity he ascribes to the removal of "fallen man." The evidence shows that the fathers thought of the statement as pertaining to human beings in the state of pure nature and in the state of fallen nature.

4.5 Second Evaluation of Lonergan's Interpretation of the Constitution

Steven A. Long criticizes "interpreters [of the constitution] for whom the certain knowledge of God by the natural light of reason is merely the faintest whiff of remote possibility."[85] Before addressing the extent to which this criticism might fruitfully be applied to Lonergan's interpretation of the constitution, it must be asked what the fathers themselves thought about the frequency of natural knowledge of God. A *relatio* by Gasser reveals an effort to avoid the matter:

> We are only talking about the principles of reason, because God can be known with certainty from the principles of reason.... We are not dealing with the exercise of reason.... [We] say nothing about the way in which man arrives at the exercise of reason.[86]

---

84. Vacant, *Études théologiques*, 1:673. Latin: "In genere de conditione naturae humanae."

85. S. Long, *Natura Pura*, 102.

86. Granderath, *Acta et Decreta*, 238–39. Latin: "Nos solummodo loquimur de principiis rationis, quod Deus ex principiis rationis certo cognosci

That the fathers did not wish to directly address the frequency of certain knowledge of God through reason, nor education's role in reason's capacity to acquire knowledge of God, leaves the door open for theologians to take a personal stance. Even the role grace might play in such knowledge is not addressed in the constitution. Lonergan has taken a personal stance on these topics—a stance that has been partially detailed above and will be detailed more fully in chapter 5 of this book. Continuing an evaluation of Lonergan's interpretation, then, involves turning the spotlight toward matters that the fathers *do* address.

One matter the fathers address is whether the formulation of the statement on natural knowledge of God should be taken as treating a *quaestio facti* or *quaestio iuris*. A note at the end of Schema II reads,

> It is not a question of *fact* . . . . What is at issue, and what the Scriptures directly affirm, is the *power* of reason: because, of course, the objective manifestation of God through creatures is directed to human reason, and [it] has the powers *to be able* to know God from that manifestation.[87]

On the surface, this note stands as evidence in support of Lonergan's interpretation, but his claim is more than simply the fathers not having engaged a *quaestio facti*. Recall that in *Method in Theology*, he claims the constitution "does not commit itself either to saying that the possibility [of the light of reason reaching certain knowledge of God] ever was realized or to predicting that it ever would be realized." Lonergan makes a similar claim, which is worth reproducing, during a 1970 interview: "What was defined in Vatican I is not that anyone ever proved, or ever will prove, the

---

possit. . . . Non agimus de exercitio rationis. . . . Nihil dicimus de via qua homo ad exercitium rationis pervenit." Attention is drawn to this material in Kerr, "Knowing God by Reason," 222.

87. Mansi, *Sacrorum Conciliorum*, 50:76–77; emphasis in original. Latin: "Non est quaestio de *facto*. . . . Id de quo agitur, et quod Scripturae immediate affirmant, est *potentia* rationis: quod nimirum obiectiva Dei per creaturas manifestatio ordinatur ad humanam rationem, et huic insunt vires, ut *possit* ex illa manifestatione Deum cognoscere."

existence of God."[88] Together, these statements sway enough in the direction of a "faintest whiff" interpretation of the constitution to warrant—and expect potential fruit from—bringing Long's criticism into contact with Lonergan.

At the heart of Long's criticism is an appeal to a canon. As it happens, it is the same canon Lonergan appropriated to justify his interpretation of the constitution. Once again, the canon reads,

> If anyone shall have said that the one true God, our Creator and our Lord, cannot be known with certitude by those things which have been made, by the natural light of human reason: let him be anathema.[89]

The construal of "cannot" above as "merely the denial of *logical* possibility ... or ... as a denial of real possibility so remote as to be irrelevant" is widely diffused, according to Long.[90] He does not invoke names. To such individuals, Long asks: Would you treat "cannot" in a nearby canon the same way? That canon reads,

> If anyone shall have said that man cannot be drawn by divine power to a knowledge and perfection which is above the natural, but that he of himself can and ought to reach the possession of all truth and good by a continual progress: let him be anathema.[91]

Long's argument differs from Lonergan's in that it does not rely on *relata* or other explanatory texts from the council but rather coherence of interpretation. Returning to the canon regarding natural knowledge of God, Long writes,

> Why should we not interpret the sense of "cannot" as pertaining, not merely to logical possibility or even

---

88. Lonergan, "Interview," 225.

89. DB 1806; DS 3026. Long employs a nearly identical translation of the canon found in Tanner, *Decrees of Ecumenical Councils*, 2:810. As for Lonergan, he reproduces it in the original Latin.

90. S. Long, *Natura Pura*, 102; emphasis in original.

91. DB 1808; DS 3028. Gasser reports that the second canon condemns "the older deists or rationalists" (Granderath, *Acta et Decreta*, 151). Latin: "Damnantur in secundo canone deistae seu rationalistae ... antiquioris."

> remote real possibility, but as the obvious "can" of proximate potency *inasmuch as the document is directive in nature*? Directive documents do not tend to waste much breath about what is scarcely possible, but do tend to concern themselves with what is achievable in the actual order of things.[92]

This raises the question whether material from the council supports Long's argument as considered here.[93] While not a case of direct support, a note attached to Schema IV lends credence to this argument insofar as it forces a question to be asked. The note reads,

> This definition, that God can be known with certainty through created things in the light of reason, and the canon corresponding to it seemed necessary, not only because of traditionalism but also because of the widespread error, that the existence of God cannot be proven by any firm evidence and therefore cannot be known with certainty.[94]

Why would the same fathers who are alarmed by those who say that the existence of God cannot be proven be noncommittal when it comes to whether the existence of God being proven "ever was

---

92. S. Long, *Natura Pura*, 102–3; emphasis in original.

93. Only those elements of Long's argument with a bearing on Lonergan's interpretation of the constitution are considered here. There are other elements of Long's argument, such as his view of "the clear words of the canon regarding God *as creator*" (S. Long, *Natura Pura*, 103; emphasis in original). These elements merit evaluation but that task is outside the scope of this book. Such an evaluation would have to wrestle, for example, with this observation attached to Schema IV: "Although the word creator is read in the canon[,] it is not therefore determined that creation can be demonstrated by reason properly so called" (Mansi, *Sacrorum Conciliorum*, 51:39). Latin: "Etsi in canone legatur vocabulum creator[,] non ideo definitur, creationem proprie dictam ratione demonstrari posse."

94. Mansi, *Sacrorum Conciliorum*, 51:39. Latin: "Definitio haec, Deum per res creatas rationis lumine certo cognosci posse, et canon ei respondens necessaria visa sunt, non solum propter traditionalismum sed etiam propter errorem late serpentem, Dei existentiam nullis firmis argumentis probari nec proinde ratione certo cognosci."

realized or . . . ever would be realized"? What weakens Lonergan's interpretation is not finding the statement on natural knowledge of God to be meager but overemphasizing that meagerness. Using this lens, which Long's criticism provides, one can see the constitution in a more balanced light.

5

Lonergan on Acts That Lead to Faith

THE PRECEDING CHAPTER OF this book attended to Lonergan's interpretation of *Dei Filius* (hereafter, the constitution). It explored what he takes the constitution to mean when it states, "God, the beginning and end of all things, can be known with certitude by the natural light of human reason from created things."[1] This chapter attends to Lonergan's views on the more multifaceted topic of the role of reason in the lead-up to religious faith—in short, the topic of acts that lead to faith.

Believing that God exists is plainly one of the acts that leads to faith,[2] but there are also acts that "attain to the certainty of the revealed fact" and "conclude that the contents of revelation are worthy of belief."[3] If this were not enough to deem the topic more multifaceted, the fathers of the council left it up to theologians to particularize such acts—to posit an account of them.

---

1. DB 1785; DS 3004.

2. This belief could conform to the declaration on natural knowledge of God (certain knowledge resulting from reflection on created things using the light of reason), or it could be the fruit of prudent conviction. That the latter could serve as an act that leads to faith is a key reason for considering Lonergan's views on the topic separately from his interpretation of the declaration on natural knowledge of God.

3. Fisichella, "Credibility," 195.

LONERGAN ON ACTS THAT LEAD TO FAITH

Three texts in which Lonergan posits an account of acts that lead to faith will be reviewed in this chapter. Section 1 takes up "Analysis of Faith," a set of notes that dates to 1951–52. These notes depict the thought of the early Lonergan on acts that lead to faith. Section 2 will discuss two new emphases in Lonergan's later writings that help explain the development one observes in his later view of such acts. The texts that represent his later view, covered in section 3, include *Method in Theology*, published in 1972, and "Variations in Fundamental Theology," a public lecture delivered in 1973.

It should be noted that the development one observes between section 1 and section 3 is explained by more than just the two new emphases to be discussed (identifying them now is not prudent). The "more" is, above all else, the Second Vatican Council. Prior to the council, theologians were discussing the sense in which a theology of faith could be built either from an analytic and abstract point of view or a synthetic and concrete point of the view.[4] The latter view was judged to be that found in the Bible. When the Second Vatican Council took place, "[its] singularly pastoral perspective signaled a recovery of the biblical understanding."[5] And markers of the adoption of that understanding appear throughout the documents promulgated. For example, Dulles calls attention to the fact that the *Dogmatic Constitution on Divine Revelation* (*Dei Verbum*) "[discusses] natural knowledge of God after revealed knowledge, reversing the order of Vatican I."[6]

Without discounting the influence on Lonergan of the currents described above, this chapter attends only to the two new emphases. The rationale for doing so is that they impact, of necessity, Lonergan's envisagement of acts that lead to faith. That is, even if Lonergan were to abandon his specifically Catholic faith, the new emphases would still exert influence on his stance on such

---

4. Fisichella, "Credibility," 196. Fisichella states that he draws the distinction from Mouroux, *Je crois en Toi*, 8. On the wider context of the discussion, see Mettepenningen, "*Nouvelle Théologie*."

5. Fisichella, "Credibility," 196.

6. Dulles, *Assurance*, 140.

acts. The sense in which this is the case will become clearer when the emphases are examined in section 2 of this chapter, and when the mature—that is, the later—Lonergan's stance is critiqued in section 4.

It is worth underlining that what will occur in section 4 is a critique, not simply an evaluation of an interpretation, since the unfolding of acts that lead to faith receives little explication in the constitution. The fathers granted theologians the freedom to posit accounts of the acts, which can be assessed using the additional lenses of clarity and prudence.

5.1 The Early Lonergan on Acts That Lead to Faith

"Analysis of Faith" is a set of notes that Lonergan prepared for students enrolled in a 1951–52 course.[7] In the notes, Lonergan explicates "acts that ... lead to faith."[8] Jonsson holds that the notes "might be regarded as Lonergan's attempt to understand the First Vatican Council's constitution ... in terms of the cognitional theory presented in *Insight*."[9] To avoid any confusion regarding this claim, note that Lonergan "began composing the text of *Insight* in the summer of 1949, finishing it in 1953."[10]

Early on in "Analysis of Faith," Lonergan explains that such an analysis "aims at resolving the assent of faith into all of its causes, intrinsic and extrinsic, proximate, intermediate, and immediate or

---

7. The course was taught at Regis College, Toronto. Details about the composition of the notes are given by Michael Shields at the outset of Lonergan, "Analysis of Faith."

8. Lonergan, "Analysis of Faith," 142. The notes belong to a category of reflection that Fisichella depicts as follows: "Under the name *analysis fidei* one may gather all the attempts that have tried to describe the theological doctrine concerning the understanding of the act of faith as a typically human act, but yet one involving grace given to the subject in order to complete an act that of itself requires divine intervention so as to raise it to knowledge of the transcendent mystery of God" ("Credibility," 195–96).

9. Jonsson, *Foundations for Knowing God*, 125.

10. Mathews, *Lonergan's Quest*, 9.

first causes."[11] He carries this out in the way that one would expect from a handout for students: He jumps into topics with little context provided, and he restates things in a more succinct fashion. The review that follows is written from the standpoint of the end of the notes, looking back.

The notes begin with a description of what Lonergan deems the *logical* faith process. It involves the following syllogism:

> Whatever God knows and truthfully reveals to humankind is to be believed by us; and if that which is to be believed exceeds the natural proportion of the human intellect, then we are in fact ordered and destined to a supernatural end. But this is something that God knows and truthfully reveals to humankind, and it certainly contains truths that are beyond the natural proportion of the human intellect. Therefore we are in fact ordered to a supernatural end, and hence all of divine revelation, including the mysteries, ought to be believed by us.[12]

Lonergan goes on to discuss what he deems the *psychological* faith process; it has two components. The first component is a set of acts that "remotely lead to faith";[13] they are the judgments by which one affirms the truth of the premises expressed in the syllogism above.[14] Lonergan holds that these judgments "do not exceed the natural proportion of the human intellect" and "are not supernatural as to their substance."[15] The same can be said of any of the acts that lead here, such as the act of affirming the existence of God. With respect to the involvement of grace, he asserts that "the

---

11. Lonergan, "Analysis of Faith," 130.

12. Lonergan, "Analysis of Faith," 126; indentations removed. Strictly speaking, the logical faith process involves two syllogisms, which are detailed on the first page of the notes. For the sake of simplicity, only the combined version of the syllogisms that Lonergan provides has been reproduced here.

13. Lonergan, "Analysis of Faith," 142.

14. Lonergan, "Analysis of Faith," 140. Elsewhere in the notes, Lonergan mentions "how gravely mistaken one would be who . . . would evaluate and judge the faith process solely on the basis of a logical analysis" (130).

15. Lonergan, "Analysis of Faith," 140–41.

remote phase in the process does not in itself require grace,"[16] but "according to the different needs of individuals, [healing] grace is required."[17]

The second component of the psychological faith process is a set of acts that "more immediately lead to faith."[18] For these acts, "the absolutely supernatural graces of enlightenment and inspiration are required."[19] It is worth reproducing Lonergan's description of these acts in full:

> First, the supernatural beginning of faith. It consists of a reflective act of understanding in which one grasps that there is sufficient evidence for reasonably eliciting [the] next five acts. Second, a practical judgment on the credibility of the mysteries. This consists in affirming that one is in fact ordered and destined to a supernatural end and that therefore belief in the mysteries of faith is a good for that person. Third, a practical judgment on the "credendity" of the mysteries. By this judgment one affirms that the whole of revelation, the mysteries included, ought to be believed. Fourth, willing the end. In this act one wills the supernatural end to which one is destined, and intends to pursue it. Fifth, willing the means. This is the "devout inclination to believe." One acknowledges one's obligation to believe, and commands an assent of faith. Sixth, the assent of faith itself elicited in the intellect and freely commanded by the will.[20]

Something must be said regarding the first and third acts. Regarding the first, Lonergan goes on to quote the constitution and state that faith is not "blind"[21] precisely because of this initial act of reflective understanding.[22] In *Insight*, Lonergan states that reflective

16. Lonergan, "Analysis of Faith," 145.
17. Lonergan, "Analysis of Faith," 142.
18. Lonergan, "Analysis of Faith," 126.
19. Lonergan, "Analysis of Faith," 144.
20. Lonergan, "Analysis of Faith," 126–27; indentations removed.
21. DB 1791; DS 3010.
22. Lonergan, "Analysis of Faith," 128. Attention is drawn to this material in Jonsson, *Foundations for Knowing God*, 125.

understanding "grasps the sufficiency of the evidence for a prospective judgment."[23] This operation is distinct from other, antecedent operations that are located under the heading of understanding, including "direct understanding,"[24] which answers questions such as "What? and Why? and How often?"[25] and conception, wherein "insights... are expressed or formulated in concepts, suppositions, definitions, postulates, hypotheses, theories."[26] What is pertinent here is the mere fact of Lonergan's making reflective understanding a part of acts that more immediately lead to faith; it shows that he adheres to the constitution while also meeting a problem of modern philosophy. As Mathews explains,

> It was Lonergan's . . . view that Fichte, Schelling, and Hegel wrote their enormous systems because in order for judgment to be possible you had to know everything about everything. . . . Reflective understanding . . . can grasp the virtually unconditioned without having to understand everything about everything.[27]

Even if details are not provided in the notes, the appearance of the operation in them corroborates Jonsson's earlier-mentioned claim that they mark Lonergan's attempt to understand the constitution against the backdrop of the cognitional theory advanced in *Insight*. And the constitution does in fact leave the door open for theologians to take a personal stance on the process of finding sufficient evidence to elicit a judgment on the credibility of the mysteries of faith.

---

23. Lonergan, *Insight*, 304. Lonergan remarks that his conception of the act is indebted to John Henry Newman: "His illative sense later became my reflective act of understanding" ("*Insight*: Revisited," 263). On this debt, see Mathews, *Lonergan's Quest*, 246.

24. Lonergan, *Insight*, 509.

25. Lonergan, *Insight*, 298.

26. Lonergan, *Insight*, 278.

27. Mathews, *Lonergan's Quest*, 46. Lonergan writes, "There is a *B if A*. Experiential objectivity gives you the *A*. The two combined give a virtually unconditioned, and that is what reflective understanding grasps. When you grasp the virtually unconditioned, you judge; you say, 'It is so'" ("Philosophical Positions," 229; emphasis in original).

Regarding the third act, one finds here an invocation of the technical term "credendity." Fisichella explains that in theological manuals, what follows the *motivum credibilitatis* is the *motivum credenditatis*. The former "allows one to conclude that the contents of revelation are worthy of belief," and the later "is the reason in terms of which one *must* believe and thus give assent to revelation."[28] Lonergan goes on to refer to credendity in conjunction with reflective understanding several times, once again showing his effort to embrace tradition while meeting modern challenges. Such an effort groups Lonergan with other modern theologians who develop the concept of credendity, such as Ambroise Gardeil (d. 1931) and Pierre Rousselot (d. 1915).[29] One disputed subject among these theologians is the level of the involvement of grace in credibility, in contrast to credendity. As seen above, Lonergan holds that the graces of enlightenment and inspiration are involved in both.

There are three points of interest in the remainder of "Analysis of Faith," as far as acts that lead to faith are concerned. The first point of interest is that Lonergan intermittently refers to the motives of credibility. It is worth once again reproducing the statement in the constitution regarding them:

> In order that the "obedience" of our faith should be "consonant with reason" [cf. Rom 12:1], God has willed that to the internal aids of the Holy Spirit there should be joined external proofs of His revelation, namely: divine facts, especially miracles and prophecies which, because they clearly show forth the omnipotence and infinite knowledge of God, are most certain signs of a divine revelation, and are suited to the intelligence of all [can. 3 and 4].[30]

In addition to miracles and prophecies, the constitution later specifies that "the Church itself ... is a very great and perpetual

---

28. Fisichella, "Credibility," 195; emphasis in original.

29. For a brief but well-contextualized summary of their accounts, see Dupont, *Phenomenology in French Philosophy*, 205–6. See also Boersma, "Sacramental Journey."

30. DB 1790; DS 3009.

motive of credibility."³¹ Now, Lonergan registers that "according to Vatican I, . . . the very fact of revelation is known through external signs, . . . which everyone can understand."³² He then puts forth a view not stated in the constitution: "The fact of revelation can be known by the natural light of reason."³³

The second point of interest concerns the preambles of faith. Lonergan writes, "By the 'preambles' we mean those foundations of faith that are known with certitude but not by divine faith."³⁴ Based on an ensuing reference to the constitution,³⁵ it can be inferred that for the early Lonergan, the existence of God, the authority of God who reveals, and the fact of revelation are known with certitude.³⁶ And they are able to be known that way by "those who go from being unbelievers to believers" and by "those who have already accepted the faith."³⁷

The third and final point of interest is Lonergan's list of "steps by which the unbeliever is led to faith."³⁸ The first step involves learning "various natural sciences, philosophy, natural theology, history, ethical conduct, and so forth." In the second step, the unbeliever investigates "the Old and New Testaments, . . . miracles and prophecies, the history of the church and the councils, and so on." Lonergan asserts that such a person "seeks all naturally knowable truth, nothing more."³⁹ He also stipulates that for these two steps, "the action of divine providence . . . is sufficient, along with the healing graces that respond to the needs of each individual."⁴⁰

---

31. DB 1794; DS 3013.

32. Lonergan, "Analysis of Faith," 149.

33. Lonergan, "Analysis of Faith," 149.

34. Lonergan, "Analysis of Faith," 147.

35. The reference is to the sentence "right reasoning demonstrates the basis of faith" (DB 1799; DS 3019).

36. These three items are what the fathers mean by "the basis of faith" (Garrigou-Lagrange, *God*, 1:25).

37. Lonergan, "Analysis of Faith," 148.

38. Lonergan, "Analysis of Faith," 142.

39. Lonergan, "Analysis of Faith," 143.

40. Lonergan, "Analysis of Faith," 144. That healing grace suffices for

In the third step, the unbeliever "is not convinced of the fact of revelation" but possesses the "'devout inclination to believe' by which he wants to believe the mysteries of faith on account of the authority of God."[41] One cannot but notice that "devout inclination to believe" is placed in quotation marks. Lonergan did the same when he employed this phrase to describe the fifth act that more immediately leads to faith. The reason for the quotation marks is, in part, the fact that the concept of *pius credulitatis affectus* is a long-standing one. The other reason: an eminent employment of the term. The Second Council of Orange, held in 529, condemns anyone who says that "the inclination to believe . . . is naturally in us."[42] This third step, then, is a graced step.

In the fourth and final step, the person's "intellect is enlightened . . . to perceive that there is sufficient evidence for making a judgment about his actual supernatural end and about the obligation to believe." Lonergan clarifies that for this step, as well as for the third, "the absolutely supernatural graces of enlightenment and inspiration are required."[43]

5.2 New Emphases in the Later Lonergan

In *Method in Theology*, Lonergan identifies two "shifts" in the modern era. The first is the "shift to interiority . . . essayed in various manners from Descartes through Kant to the nineteenth-century German idealists."[44] The second is the "more emphatic shift from knowledge to faith, will, conscience, decision, action in Kierkegaard, Schopenhauer, Newman, Nietzsche, Blondel, the

---

certain acts applies to cases that are hypothetical, admits Lonergan, and such a view could be challenged by "showing that those hypothetical cases never actually exist."

41. Lonergan, "Analysis of Faith," 143.

42. DB 178; DS 375. This translation of *credulitatis affectum* has been chosen for the sake of consistency.

43. Lonergan, "Analysis of Faith," 144.

44. Lonergan, *Method in Theology*, 316.

personalists, and the existentialists."[45] This shift can summarily be called the shift to decision.

The later Lonergan embraces aspects of the shift to interiority and aspects of the shift to decision. The result is two new emphases in his later writings. To say they are new *emphases* is to register that interiority and decision were acknowledged in his early writings but not fully developed.

To understand the emphasis on interiority, one must attend to what Lonergan calls "stages of meaning." In *Method in Theology*, he delineates three such stages: common sense, theory, and interiority.[46] Although the stages are "ideal constructs" and "not chronological,"[47] Lonergan does identify when the second and third stages first arose in history. He writes, "The [Greek] discovery of mind marks the transition from the first stage of meaning to the second."[48] And Lonergan's statement above regarding Descartes and Kant historically locates the transition from the second stage of meaning to the third.

Lonergan also claims that with each stage-transition, new differentiations of consciousness emerge. His list of differentiations reads as follows: "the religious, the linguistic, the literary, the systematic, the scientific, the scholarly, and . . . intentionality analysis."[49] Henceforth the last three will be referred to collectively as *the modern differentiations*. Lonergan contends that the modern differentiations "are quite beyond the horizon of ancient Greece and medieval Europe."[50] This statement links the birth of the modern differentiations with the stage of interiority—a stage that begins, as seen above, in the time of Descartes and Kant.

---

45. Lonergan, *Method in Theology*, 316.

46. Lonergan, *Method in Theology*, 85. Thomas McPartland alerts readers to some key differences between Lonergan's stages and those that positivists propose, namely myth, metaphysics, and science (*Philosophy of Historical Existence*, 74).

47. Lonergan, *Method in Theology*, 85.

48. Lonergan, *Method in Theology*, 93.

49. Lonergan, "Philosophy of God, and Theology," 209.

50. Lonergan, *Method in Theology*, 317.

Reassessing Faith and Reason

Since Descartes and Kant were active before the First Vatican Council, the question slowly dawns regarding the extent to which the fathers adopted the modern differentiations. Lonergan's answer can be inferred from a statement in "Philosophy of God, and Theology," a lecture delivered at Gonzaga University in 1972:

> The Thomist and especially the neo-Thomist conceptions of philosophy and theology rest on the religious, the linguistic, the literary, and the systematic differentiations of consciousness. Commonly they are unfamiliar with the differentiations resulting from modern science, modern scholarship, and ... intentionality analysis.[51]

Note that the last item in this list is synonymous with the modern philosophic differentiation. Now, this statement, on its own, merely implies that one conducts philosophical and theological inquiry differently when that inquiry is shaped by the modern differentiations. There is an ensuing statement that introduces an evaluative element: "With every differentiation of consciousness the same object becomes apprehended in a different and more adequate fashion."[52]

The central topic of this chapter can now be returned to. For Lonergan, given the various claims above, a contemporary theologian who engages the modern differentiations apprehends acts that lead to faith *more adequately* than the envisagement provided in the constitution. This permits the contemporary theologian not only to read the constitution as limited in certain respects but also to interpret what it declares in light of those limitations. In Lonergan's terminology, a "transposition" of the constitution's declarations is necessary—a transposition being "a restatement of an earlier position in a new and broader context."[53] Such a restatement would include an appropriation of the modern differentiations. For Lonergan, it was the cessation of overlooking the modern

---

51. Lonergan, "Philosophy of God," 209.
52. Lonergan, "Philosophy of God," 210.
53. Lonergan, "Horizons and Transpositions," 410.

differentiations that foreshadowed the "change of attitude" towards Scholasticism at the Second Vatican Council.[54]

There remains the other new emphasis in the later Lonergan's writing: decision. Explicating this new emphasis requires taking a step back to discuss transcendental method, which Lonergan defends in the opening of *Method in Theology*. There he states that it is "a heightening of consciousness that brings to light our conscious and intentional operations."[55] He posits, and believes each person can discover, "intentional and conscious acts on ... four levels[:] ... experiencing, understanding, judging, and deciding."[56] To block their dynamism is, for Lonergan, to engage in self-sabotage. In his own words: "Alienation is man's disregard of the transcendental precepts, Be attentive, Be intelligent, Be reasonable, Be responsible."[57]

Of interest here, of course, is the fourth level. This is the level "on which we are concerned with ourselves, our own operations, our goals, and so deliberate about possible courses of action, evaluate them, decide, and carry out our decisions."[58] While Lonergan insists on "preserving the integrity of [the first three levels],"[59] he lauds the thinkers who have punctuated the fourth level.

With such thinkers—Kierkegaard, Schopenhauer, et al.—writing before the First Vatican Council, the question once again dawns regarding the fathers' embrace or rejection of the emerging focus on decision. The answer, this time, need not be inferred. When Lonergan discusses shifting one's thinking "from human nature to the existential human subject, from the conditions of possibility assured by human nature to the conditions of actuality

---

54. Lonergan, "Scope of Renewal," 283. See also Lonergan's remark, and surrounding reflection, that "it is very evident that Aristotle has been superseded" (*Method in Theology*, 310).

55. Lonergan, *Method in Theology*, 25.

56. Lonergan, *Method in Theology*, 120. Note that for Lonergan, "judgement is concerned to complete one's knowledge of what exists or is the case, whereas decision is concerned to put into effect what would not otherwise be the case" (Meynell, *Philosophy of Bernard Lonergan*, 127).

57. Lonergan, *Method in Theology*, 55.

58. Lonergan, *Method in Theology*, 9.

59. Lonergan, *Method in Theology*, 340.

permitted by the aberrations of human history," he states that "the former was the viewpoint of Vatican I."[60] A contemporary theologian who engages the fourth level of consciousness thus moves beneath or beyond—the descriptor rests on one's acceptance or rejection of the later Lonergan's project—what is presented in the constitution.

5.3 The Later Lonergan on Acts That Lead to Faith

In 1973, two decades after writing the "Analysis of Faith" notes, Lonergan delivered a public lecture entitled "Variations in Fundamental Theology" at Trinity College in Toronto.[61] Halfway through the lecture, he mentions that, according to chapter 3 of the constitution, "prophecies and miracles . . . show forth the omniscience and the omnipotence of God."[62] Lonergan then remarks,

> Today, [prophecies and miracles] have been engulfed in the mountainous extent and intricate subtlety of biblical studies and critical history. God's gift of his grace is as frequent, as powerful, but also as silent and secret as ever, while we are perturbed by the probing of depth psychology and bewildered by the claims of linguistic analysts, by the obscurities of phenomenology, by the oddities of existentialism, by the programs of economic, social, and ecological reformers, by the beckoning of ecumenists and universalists.[63]

This remark exhibits Lonergan's acknowledgment of the complexity that the modern differentiations introduce into one's envisagement of the motives of credibility.

---

60. Lonergan, "Horizons and Transpositions," 428.

61. He delivered the lecture again at Yale University in 1974.

62. Lonergan, "Variations in Fundamental Theology," 249. He does not include the adverb "clearly."

63. Lonergan, "Variations in Fundamental Theology," 249. For analysis of the ecclesial backdrop of these developments, see Latourelle, "Absence and Presence."

Lonergan goes on to ascribe "hollowness" to the logic-centered form of fundamental theology that establishes "the existence and attributes of God," followed by "man's duty of worshiping God," and so on.[64] His appraisal of an apologetics that exclusively follows this approach is divulged by a quotation he supplies from John Henry Newman (d. 1890): "Logic makes but a sorry rhetoric with the multitude; first shoot round corners and you may not despair of converting by a syllogism."[65]

Lonergan's word choice is judicious. "Hollow" implies severe lack, not complete incorrectness. Complete incorrectness would essentially overturn his early stance on acts that lead to faith. Lonergan believes the theologian can "[learn] from modern conceptions and techniques of science, of interpretation, of history . . . without any repudiation of what is valid in the Catholic past."[66]

As for what could be attended to without repudiating what is valid in the Catholic past, Lonergan points to religious experience. The fourth level of consciousness, the level of decision, is the entry point for religious experience. In "Philosophy of God, and Theology," Lonergan explains:

> The exercise of the gift [of God's love] consists in acts of love, but the gift itself is a dynamic state that fulfils the basic thrust of the human spirit to self-transcendence. That fulfilment brings a deep-set joy . . . [and] a radical peace. . . . God's gift of his love . . . does not suppose that we know God. . . . The gift occurs with indeed a determinate content but without an intellectually apprehended object. Religious experience at its root is experience of an unconditioned and unrestricted being in love. But what we are in love with remains something that we have to find out. When we find it out in the context of a philosophy, there results a philosophy of God. When we find it

---

64. Lonergan, "Variations in Fundamental Theology," 257.

65. Lonergan, *Method in Theology*, 338n3.

66. Lonergan, "Variations in Fundamental Theology," 257. "Lonergan is arguing that continuity is continuity of meaning[,] not the continuity of the exact symbolic expression (language) that expresses the meaning" (Sauer, *Lonergan's "Method in Theology,"* 139).

out in the context of a functionally differentiated theology, there results a functional specialty, systematics.[67]

When Lonergan unpacks these claims elsewhere, he regularly employs terminology from the Catholic past. For instance, in *Method in Theology*, he asserts that "the dynamic state of itself is operative grace, but the same state as principle of acts of love, hope, faith, repentance, and so on, is grace as cooperative."[68] To not repudiate the Catholic past, however, he must also evade what is anathematized in the constitution. With respect to religious experience, the constitution anathematizes anyone who claims that

> divine revelation cannot be made credible by external signs, and for this reason men ought to be moved to faith by the internal experience alone of each one, or by private inspiration.[69]

Nowhere does the later Lonergan contend that divine revelation *cannot* be made credible by external signs, or that human beings *ought* to be moved to faith by internal experience alone as an alternative. He does state that persons *can* be moved to faith by internal experience alone—in his terms, by religious experience alone, but neither the canon above or nor the remainder of the constitution condemn this. As Dulles observes,

> Although Vatican I particularly emphasized the arguments from prophecy and miracle, it did not deny that valid conclusions may be drawn from the inherent features of the Christian message judged in the light of the believer's moral and religious sense.[70]

The later Lonergan's stance on the role of religious experience is, therefore, harmonious with the constitution. Still, one wonders about the degree of harmony. It is not insignificant that the constitution "emphasizes," as Dulles puts it, miracles and prophecies.

---

67. Lonergan, "Philosophy of God," 204.
68. Lonergan, *Method in Theology*, 107.
69. DB 1812; DS 3033.
70. Dulles, *Assurance*, 210.

De-emphasizing these signs would place Lonergan in friction with—but not in disobedience to—the constitution.

Three statements can be considered in assessing the matter of friction with the constitution. First, addressing religion in general in "Philosophy of God, and Theology," Lonergan states,

> The vast majority of mankind have been religious. One cannot claim that their religion has been based on some philosophy of God. One can easily argue that their religious concern arose out of their religious experience. In that case the basic question of God is the [decision-level question "With whom are we in love?"], which arises out of religious experience.[71]

This statement depicts religion as normally based on internal experience. It is relevant to the question at hand but wanting because it is not focused on Catholic believers.

A second statement, found in a section of *Method in Theology* entitled "The Function of Systematics," is less wanting. Lonergan writes,

> With regard to the actual order in which we live, I should say that normally religious conversion precedes the effort to work out rigorous proofs for the existence of God. But I do not think it impossible that such proofs might be a factor facilitating religious conversion so that, by way of exception, certain knowledge of God's existence should precede the acceptance of God's gift of his love.[72]

Although more relevant in that it arises in a discussion of Catholic theology, this statement still remains imprecise on the frequency of certain knowledge of God prior to faith. At the very least, one gets a sense of significant rarity from the phrasing he uses above: "*I do not think it impossible* that . . . proofs *might* be a *factor* facilitating religious conversion" (emphasis added).

A third and final statement, appearing in the section "A Technical Note" in *Method in Theology*, treats apologetics. Lonergan

---

71. Lonergan, "Philosophy of God," 208.
72. Lonergan, *Method in Theology*, 339.

writes, "The apologist's task is neither to produce in others nor to justify for them God's gift of his love. . . . The apologist's task is to aid others in integrating God's gift with the rest of their living."[73] To comprehend this approach to apologetics, one must reside in a context where both interiority and decision are valued. As James Sauer explains,

> Lonergan reconfigures apologetics from an intellectual task (theory) to the existential. This is consistent with his view that religious experience (the data) initially addresses the 4th level of conscious intentionality—the existential level. One grasps this only from a stance in interiority. Before interiority is differentiated from common sense and theory, apologetics is merely practical or intellectual.[74]

Intellectual apologetics receives little acknowledgment in *Method in Theology*. The phrases "preambles of faith" and "motives of credibility" are not found in the book, and references to miracles and prophecies are few in number. These are indicators of friction with the constitution. Even when Lonergan appears to be commencing a discussion of intellectual apologetics, the discussion is cut short: "The question of God . . . may begin as a purely metaphysical question but it becomes a moral and eventually a religious question." Lonergan continues, "To deal with all of these levels requires putting an end to the isolation of philosophy of God."[75]

Ending the isolation of the philosophy of God, Lonergan admits, marks a departure from his earlier practice.[76] That is a move

73. Lonergan, *Method in Theology*, 123.

74. Sauer, Lonergan's "*Method in Theology*," 139. In the stage of interiority, "the gift of God's love first is described as an experience and only consequently is objectified in theoretical categories" (Lonergan, *Method in Theology*, 107).

75. Lonergan, "Philosophy of God," 205.

76. Looking back, Lonergan writes, "The trouble with chapter 19 in *Insight* was that it . . . treated God's existence and attributes in a purely objective fashion. It made no effort to deal with the subject's religious horizon" ("Philosophy of God," 172). Also: "In *Method* . . . our basic awareness of God comes to us not through arguments or choices but primarily through God's gift of his love" (Lonergan, "*Insight*: Revisited," 277). For comment on this development, see Hefling, "Philosophy, Theology, and God," 121.

he is free to make. Nonetheless, he admits that the move can be seen by some to "not square with the decree of the First Vatican Council [on natural knowledge of God]."[77] In his judgment, such persons have made the mistake of judging the constitution to declare "that fallen man without grace can know with certainty the existence of God." The removal of "fallen man" and other terms from Schema IV of the constitution onward proves, in Lonergan's view, that such a judgment is false. Now, Lonergan's interpretation of the constitution was already evaluated in chapter 4 of this book. What is relevant at present is not his interpretation of the document; again, the constitution has little to say on acts that lead to faith and the *later* Lonergan neither interprets the little it does say nor defies its canons pertaining to the matter. Instead, what is relevant is the degree of harmony with the constitution.

What illuminates the degree is Lonergan's acknowledgment that leaning towards an existential approach to apologetics will be taken by some to "rob pure reason of its purity."[78] This objection only holds, he argues, if one "knows . . . logic [but] does not think of method"—if one sees objectivity as "the fruit of immediate experience, of . . . necessary truths, and of rigorous inferences." This objection dissolves "when method is added to the picture," for at that point "objectivity is the fruit of authentic subjectivity, of being attentive, intelligent, reasonable, and responsible."[79] It is the upshot of adding method to the picture that illuminates the degree of harmony, for it means embracing what this chapter has referred to as the modern differentiations.[80]

Among the modern differentiations is intentionality analysis, which is marked by an abandonment of faculty psychology. It establishes "a more comprehensive, coherent, and realistic grasp of the relationship of the [cognitional] operations operating together in a full act of consciousness," writes Sauer, which in turn causes "'pure intellect' (reason) and 'will' to vanish as distinct faculties."[81] With

77. Lonergan, "Philosophy of God," 204.
78. Lonergan, "Philosophy of God," 204.
79. Lonergan, "Philosophy of God," 202.
80. Lonergan, "Philosophy of God," 209.
81. Sauer, *Lonergan's "Method in Theology,"* 138.

no pure reason to rob in the first place, according to Lonergan, an existential approach to apologetics is justified—one that prioritizes persons over propositions and decisions over of logic.[82]

A further consequence of "[moving] out of a faculty psychology . . . and into an intentionality analysis" is "the possibility of an exception to the old adage, *Nihil amatum nisi praecognitum* (Nothing can be loved that is not already known)."[83] Now, in one passage in which Lonergan reproduces and elaborates on this adage, he relates it, by way of a footnote, to the First Vatican Council. The passage in question reads,

> It may be objected that *nihil amatum nisi praecognitum*. But while that is true of other human love, it need not be true of the love with which God floods our hearts through the Holy Spirit he has given us (Rom 5:5). That grace could be the finding that grounds our seeking God through natural reason and through positive religion. It could be the touchstone by which we judge whether it is really God that natural reason reaches or positive religion preaches.[84]

A footnote affixed to this passage reads, "On the transition from the context of Vatican I to the contemporary context on natural knowledge of God, see my paper, 'Natural Knowledge of God.'" This 1968 convention paper was examined in chapter 4 of this book. What the footnote implies is that *nihil amatum nisi praecognitum* is unwavering only from the vantage point of the First Vatican Council.[85] A contemporary theologian who embraces the shift to interiority can discern exceptions to it. And concomitant with such discernment is a staggering yet easily unnoticed implication: "Philosophy is a variety of religious experience," as Thomas McPartland puts it.[86]

82. Sauer, *Lonergan's "Method in Theology,"* 274–75.
83. Lonergan, *Method in Theology*, 340.
84. Lonergan, *Method in Theology*, 278.
85. In the stream of neo-Thomism "that continues in Kleutgen's trajectory," Rowland finds a "two-tiered account of nature and grace and faith and reason" (*Catholic Theology*, 53, 75). For further analysis, see Duffy, *Graced Horizon*, 55.
86. McPartland, *Philosophy of Historical Existence*, 147.

5.4 A Critique of Lonergan on Acts That Lead to Faith

Since what is being critiqued here is largely a personal stance, the mature Lonergan—the later Lonergan—will be in focus. Nonetheless, there will be moments where setting up a contrast with his early stance aids the critique. It should also be stressed that the critique is bound up with the statistics on religion in America reviewed in this book's introduction.

To begin the critique, it is worth registering that the later Lonergan's stance is but an instance of an outlook shared, with variation, by a host of theologians following the Second Vatican Council. George Tavard provides a sketch of this outlook:

> The approach to Revelation and faith of the Constitution *Dei Filius* of [the First Vatican Council] reflected the concerns of the second half of the nineteenth century: what mattered was the rationality of faith and the acceptability of Revelation by reasonable beings. . . . The situation has changed considerably since 1870. Our contemporaries are more interested in existential and personal values than in rationality. In the realm of theological research and elaboration, the climate of the nineteenth century, which gave apologetics a central place, is all but forgotten today. Theology is now investigating Christian experience rather than the rational aspects of Revelation.[87]

To Tavard's remark that the situation has changed considerably since 1870, one could confidently respond that the situation has changed considerably since 1966. To his remark that what mattered was the rationality of faith and the acceptability of Revelation by reasonable beings, one could confidently respond that the present tense ought to be used instead. These responses are supported

---

87. Tavard, "Commentary on *De Revelatione*," 12–13. Joseph Ratzinger (before being elected pope) contends that the concept of miracles and prophecies as external proofs "is given a notably more modest place [in the Second Vatican Council's *Dei Verbum*]; faith appears as more inwardly orientated, and no further attempt is made to make the certainty of faith measurable by positivist criteria" (Ratzinger, "*Dogmatic Constitution*: Chapter 1," 3:178).

Reassessing Faith and Reason

by what was discussed in the introduction of this book: three mid-2000s bestsellers that deem religious faith not compatible with human reason and Pew statistics showing this view to be widely held among religious "nones" in America.

One might assume a critique of the later Lonergan to involve no more than duplicating the responses above. What Tavard offers, however, is merely a rough summation of a sentiment shared after the Second Vatican Council. The later Lonergan offers a highly nuanced stance on acts that lead to faith. This alone would warrant a cautious rather than rash response, but an additional ground for doing so is the inexactness referred to at the outset of this chapter. To elaborate, and to give an example, the fathers declare that "right reasoning demonstrates the basis of faith"[88] but do not spell out what this reasoning entails.[89] To give another example, the fathers declare that miracles and prophecies "clearly show forth the omnipotence and infinite knowledge of God"[90] but do not specify the manner in which one grasps that they "show" this.

Before commencing the critique itself, it is useful to ponder an outline, composed by Fisichella, of the function of the motives in the constitution:

> The council introduces the theme of the signs of revelation [miracles, prophecies] as the form that allows the act of faith to correspond to the demands of reason.... These signs are presented by the council as elements that can guarantee the credibility of that which comes to be expounded; therefore they are given as contents that, while they come to be known by reason according to its

---

88. DB 1799; DS 3019.

89. Recall that "demonstration" is not used in a technical manner here. See Granderath, *Acta et Decreta*, 204. Furthermore, "right reasoning" is rather nebulous; it has several meanings in Aquinas, for example. See Lisska, "Right Reason," 163–64.

90. DB 1790; DS 3009. It is worth noting here an error in a widely used translation of the constitution: "clearly demonstrating as they do the omnipotence and infinite knowledge of God" (Tanner, *Decrees of Ecumenical Councils*, 2:807). The word "demonstrating" does not appear in the original; it reads, "Dei omnipotentiam et infinitam scientiam luculenter commonstrent" (Mansi, *Sacrorum Conciliorum*, 51:432).

own laws, yet are equally fitted to be believed and accepted through an act of the will.[91]

The element of this outline that will ultimately bring to light the weakness of the later Lonergan's stance is the capacity of the signs to satiate "the demands of reason."

Recall from this book's introduction that 49 percent of "nones" who left religion behind did so on the bases of "science," "common sense," "logic," and "a lack of evidence."[92] It should be acknowledged, of course, that these terms are employed with differing levels of precision. Few of those who answered "science," for example, will have assessed the rival theories of scientific method.[93] Even fewer will have assessed the rival metamethods used to choose one.[94] Nevertheless, some generalizations can be made about the "nones" who employ the terms above. They do not wish their reason to be robbed of its purity. They do not want to be informed that it would be an exception for them to know God with certainty before accepting God's gift of his love. They do not wish to encounter an apologist whose goal is to aid them in integrating God's gift with the rest of their living. At best, these suggestions will result in indifference toward faith; at worst, indignation.

Imagine, for a moment, bringing these existential-apologetic attitudes to an unbeliever who subscribes to some version of Clifford's principle: "It is wrong always, everywhere, and for any one, to believe anything upon insufficient evidence."[95] Not only is such a person being asked to overlook the desire for evidence on the way to faith; he or she must forgo the desire again at the end of the path. As Lonergan himself asserts, "the assent of faith" is assent to "the religious community's confession of the mysteries . . .

---

91. Fisichella, "Credibility," 195.

92. Lipka, "America's 'Nones,'" para. 3.

93. See Nola and Sankey, *Theories of Scientific Method*, 83.

94. To appreciate their complexity, consider that these metamethods can be a priori, empirical, conventionalist, pragmatist, decision theoretical, or nihilistic (Nola and Sankey, *Theories of Scientific Method*, 81).

95. Clifford, "Ethics of Belief," 295.

hidden in God."[96] Further still, such a person is likely to see him or herself forgoing autonomy, at least as it is commonly conceived of today. That conception is summed up by Linda Zagzebski: "If a person acts or believes on authority, [he or she] is not acting as a self[-]governing person should act.... So one's autonomy can be violated by oneself as well as by other persons."[97] To an unbeliever already uneasy about the motive of faith, namely, the authority of God revealing, an apologetic approach that deems "hollow" the provision of evidence of that authority is imprudent.

The early Lonergan's stance on acts that lead to faith is more suited to the typical unbeliever as identified by the Pew statistics. Designating that stance as compatible with an intellectual apologetics is supported, first and foremost, by the mere fleshing out of "steps by which the unbeliever is led to faith."[98] Beyond this, there are Lonergan's characterizations of acts that remotely lead to faith. They "do not exceed the natural proportion of the human intellect"; they "are not supernatural as to their substance";[99] they are part of a process that "does not in itself require grace."[100] Even so simple a thing as the early Lonergan's claim that "the fact of revelation can be known by the natural light of reason"[101] meshes with, rather than resists, an intellectual apologetics.

Alongside this support for an intellectual apologetics is a degree of innovation. Lonergan integrates a reflective act of understanding into his account of acts that lead to faith. Involving supernatural grace, and overcoming the modern requirement of exhaustive knowledge for a judgment, the early Lonergan tackles the conditions of the preambles of faith without endorsing an existential apologetics. As a consequence, the early Lonergan does not enter into friction with the constitution.

---

96. Lonergan, *Method in Theology*, 349.
97. Zagzebski, "Defense of Religious Authority," 17.
98. Lonergan, "Analysis of Faith," 142–44.
99. Lonergan, "Analysis of Faith," 140–41.
100. Lonergan, "Analysis of Faith," 145.
101. Lonergan, "Analysis of Faith," 142.

Conclusion

THE VIEW THAT RELIGIOUS faith is not compatible with human reason was popular enough in the middle of the aughts to land three books espousing it on the *New York Times* bestsellers list. It was not until the Pew Research Center conducted large-scale surveys on religion, however, that the popularity of the view could be quantified. As outlined in this book's introduction, surveys showed substantial growth between 2007 and 2014 in the number of Americans who claim to be atheist, agnostic, or "nothing in particular." And the view that faith is not compatible with reason, according to a survey conducted in 2016, was the main basis for persons raised in a religion to become a "none." It was the steady growth of reason-based "nones," in particular, that motivated the authoring of this book.

Among the possible responses to the increase of reason-based "nones" is opposition, where one challenges the view that faith and reason are incompatible. As explained in the introduction, opposition is not a suitable response towards a view whose status has shifted from outlier to mainstream. The appropriate response is a reassessment of the view articulated in one's own tradition. For its part, this book reassesses the articulation found in Roman Catholicism. Reassessment, as explained, is the exploration of a matter with a sharper expectation of clarity and a focus on under-investigated aspects. It is hoped that this book makes a useful contribution to the project of reassessment. To be useful, it should engender a sense of the complexity of holding that faith and reason *are* compatible, making any future opposition to the view that they are not compatible more precise.

Bibliography

Alfaro, Juan. "Preambles of Faith." In *Encyclopedia of Theology*, edited by Karl Rahner, 512–14. London: Burns and Oates, 1975.

Ameriks, Karl. *Kant and the Historical Turn: Philosophy as Critical Interpretation.* Oxford: Clarendon, 2006.

Aquinas, Thomas. *Summa Contra Gentiles.* Translated by Anton C. Pegis et al. 4 vols. in 5 bks. Garden City, NY: Image, 1955–57.

———. *Summa Theologica.* Translated by the Fathers of the English Dominican Province. 3 vols. New York: Benziger Brothers, 1947–48.

Atlas, Samuel. "Jacobi, Friedrich Heinrich." In *Encyclopedia of Philosophy*, edited by Donald M. Borchert, 4:769–73. 2nd ed. Detroit: Gale, 2006.

Aubert, Roger. *Le problème de l'acte de foi: Données traditionnelles et résultats des controverses récentes.* Louvain: Warny, 1958.

———. *Vatican I.* Paris: Orante, 1964.

Augustine of Hippo. *The Trinity.* Translated by Stephen McKenna. Washington, DC: Catholic University of America Press, 1963.

Barbour, Ian G. "On Typologies for Relating Science and Religion." *Zygon* 37 (2002) 345–59.

———. *Religion and Science: Historical and Contemporary Issues.* San Francisco: HarperSanFrancisco, 1997.

Basinger, Randall. "Faith/Reason Typologies: A Constructive Proposal." *Christian Scholar's Review* 27 (1997) 62–73.

Baur, Michael. "Kant, Lonergan, and Fichte on the Critique of Immediacy and the Epistemology of Constraint in Human Knowing." *International Philosophical Quarterly* 43 (2003) 91–112.

Bautain, Louis. "A Letter on How God's Existence Cannot be Proved." In *Romance and the Rock: Nineteenth-Century Catholics on Faith and Reason*, edited by Joseph Fitzer, 153–66. Minneapolis: Fortress, 1989.

———. *Philosophie du christianisme: Correspondance religieuse de L. Bautain.* 2 vols. Paris: Dérivaux, 1835.

Bibliography

———. *Philosophie: Psychologie expérimentale*. 2 vols. Strasbourg: Derivaux, 1839.

———. *Résumé des conférences faites au cercle catholique, 1842–43*. Paris: Cercle Catholique, 1843.

Boersma, Hans. "A Sacramental Journey to the Beatific Vision: The Intellectualism of Pierre Rousselot." *HeyJ* 49 (2008) 1015–34.

Bokenkotter, Thomas. *A Concise History of the Catholic Church*. Rev. ed. New York: Image, 1990.

Bradley, Denis J. M. "Transcendental Critique and Realist Metaphysics." *Thomist* 39 (1975) 631–67.

Braxton, Edward K. "Knowledge of God in Bernard Lonergan and Hans Küng." *HTR* 70 (1977) 327–41.

Butler, Cuthbert. *The Vatican Council, 1869–1870: Based on Bishop Ullathorne's Letters*. Edited by Christopher Butler. Westminster, MD: Newman, 1962.

Byrne, Patrick H. "God and the Statistical Universe." *Zygon* 16 (1981) 345–63.

Catholic Church. *Catechism of the Catholic Church*. 2nd ed. Vatican City: Vaticana, 2019.

Chossat, Marcel. "Dieu (Connaissance naturelle de)." In *Dictionnaire de théologie catholique: Contenant l'exposé des doctrines de la théologie catholique*, edited by Alfred Vacant, 4.1:756–874. 15 vols. in 30 bks. Paris: Letouzey et Ané, 1923–50.

Clifford, W. K. "The Ethics of Belief." *Contemporary Review* 29 (1877) 289–309.

Coffey, David M. "Natural Knowledge of God: Reflections on Romans 1:18–32." *TS* 31 (1970) 674–91.

Congregation for the Doctrine of the Faith. "Doctrinal Commentary on the Concluding Formula of the *Professio Fidei*." Vatican, June 29, 1998. https://www.vatican.va/roman_curia/congregations/cfaith/documents/rc_con_cfaith_doc_1998_professio-fidei_en.html.

Cooperman, Alan, et al. *When Americans Say They Believe in God, What Do They Mean?* Pew Research, Apr. 25, 2018. https://www.pewresearch.org/religion/2018/04/25/when-americans-say-they-believe-in-god-what-do-they-mean.

Crawford, Alexander W. *The Philosophy of F. H. Jacobi*. New York: Macmillan, 1905.

Cronin, Brian. *Foundations of Philosophy: Lonergan's Cognitional Theory and Epistemology*. Nairobi: Consolata Institute of Philosophy Press, 1999.

Davies, Brian. *Thomas Aquinas's "Summa Contra Gentiles": A Guide and Commentary*. New York: Oxford University Press, 2016.

Dawkins, Richard. *The God Delusion*. London: Bantam, 2006.

Deufel, Konrad. *Kirche und Tradition*. Paderborn: Schöningh, 1976.

Duffy, Stephen J. *The Graced Horizon: Nature and Grace in Modern Catholic Thought*. Collegeville, MN: Liturgical, 1992.

Dulles, Avery. *The Assurance of Things Hoped For: A Theology of Christian Faith*. New York: Oxford University Press, 1994.

Bibliography

———. "Faith and Reason: From Vatican I to John Paul II." In *The Two Wings of Catholic Thought: Essays on "Fides et Ratio,"* edited by David Ruel Foster and Joseph W. Koterski, 193–208. Washington, DC: Catholic University of America Press, 2003.

———. *A History of Apologetics.* 2nd ed. San Francisco: Ignatius, 2005.

Dupont, Christian. *Phenomenology in French Philosophy: Early Encounters.* Phaenomenologica 208. New York: Springer, 2014.

Fisichella, Rino. "Credibility." In *Dictionary of Fundamental Theology,* edited by René Latourelle and Rino Fisichella, 193–209. English ed. edited by René Latourelle. New York: Crossroad, 1994.

Francis. *Lumen Fidei.* San Francisco: Ignatius, 2013.

Fries, Heinrich. "Faith and Knowledge." In *Encyclopedia of Theology,* edited by Karl Rahner, 518–24. London: Burns and Oates, 1975.

Gaillardetz, Richard R. "What the Church Teaches: Gradations of Church Doctrine." In *Teaching with Authority: A Theology of the Magisterium in the Church,* 101–28. Theology and Life 41. Collegeville, MN: Liturgical, 1997.

Gardner, Sebastian. *Kant and the "Critique of Pure Reason."* Routledge Philosophy GuideBooks. New York: Routledge, 1999.

Garrigou-Lagrange, Réginald. *God: His Existence and His Nature.* Translated by Bede Rose. 2 vols. St. Louis: Herder, 1946–47.

Geiselmann, Josef Rupert. *The Meaning of Tradition.* Translated by W. J. O'Hara. New York: Herder and Herder, 1966.

Gilson, Étienne. *Being and Some Philosophers.* 2nd ed. Toronto: Pontifical Institute of Mediaeval Studies, 1952.

Gram, Moltke S. "Intellectual Intuition: The Continuity Thesis." *Journal of the History of Ideas* 42 (1981) 287–304.

———. "Things in Themselves: The Historical Lessons." *Journal of the History of Philosophy* 18 (1980) 407–31.

Granderath, Theodor, ed. *Acta et Decreta Sacrosancti Oecumenici Concilii Vaticani cum Perultis Aliis Documentis ad Concilium Ejusque Historiam Spectanibus.* Freiburg: Herder, 1892.

———. *Histoire du Concile du Vatican: Depuis sa première annonce jusqu'à sa prorogation, d'après les documents authentiques.* 4 vols. in 6 bks. Brussels: Dewit, 1907–14.

Grier, Michelle. *Kant's Doctrine of Transcendental Illusion.* New York: Cambridge University Press, 2001.

Guarino, Thomas. "Vatican I and Dogmatic Apophasis: Historical and Theological Reflections." *ITQ* 61 (1995) 70–82.

Günther, Anton. "A Letter on Human Knowledge and the Divine Trinity." Translation of Letter 11 in *Vorschule zur speculativen Theologie des positiven Christenthums.* In *Romance and the Rock: Nineteenth-Century Catholics on Faith and Reason,* edited by Joseph Fitzer, 136–52. Minneapolis: Fortress, 1989.

Bibliography

———. *Vorschule zur speculativen Theologie des positiven Christenthums*. 2 vols. 2nd ed. Vienna: Wallishausser, 1846–48.
Günther, Anton, and J. H. Pabst. *Janusköpfe für Philosophie und Theologie*. Vienna: Wallishausser, 1834.
Guyer, Paul. *Kant*. Routledge Philosophers. New York: Routledge, 2006.
Haffner, Paul. *The Mystery of Reason*. Leominster, MA: Gracewing, 2001.
Harris, Sam. *The End of Faith: Religion, Terror, and the Future of Reason*. New York: Norton, 2004.
———. *The End of Faith: Religion, Terror, and the Future of Reason*. [Paperback.] New York: Norton, 2005.
Hefling, Charles C., Jr. "Philosophy, Theology, and God." In *The Desires of the Human Heart: An Introduction to the Theology of Bernard Lonergan*, edited by Vernon Gregson, 120–43. New York: Paulist, 1988.
Helm, Paul, ed., *Faith and Reason*. Oxford Readers. Oxford: Oxford University Press, 1999.
Hennesey, James J. "Vatican Council I." In *New Catholic Encyclopedia*, edited by Faculty of the Catholic University of America, 14:403–7. 2nd ed. Detroit: Gale, 2003.
Hitchens, Christopher. *God Is Not Great: How Religion Poisons Everything*. New York: Twelve, 2007.
Horton, Walter Marshall. *The Philosophy of the Abbé Bautain*. New York: New York University Press, 1926.
Inglis, John. *Spheres of Philosophical Inquiry and the Historiography of Medieval Philosophy*. Brill's Studies in Intellectual History 81. Leiden: Brill, 1998.
Jacobi, Friedrich Heinrich. *Friedrich Heinrich Jacobi's Werke*. 6 vols. Leipzig: Fleischer, 1812–25.
———. *The Main Philosophical Writings and the Novel "Allwill."* Translated and edited by George Di Giovanni. Montreal: McGill University Press, 2009.
Jaramillo, Alicia. "The Necessity of Raising the Question of God: Aquinas and Lonergan on the Quest After Complete Intelligibility." *Thomist* 71 (2007) 221–67.
John Paul II. "*Fidei Depositum*: On the Publication of the Catechism of the Catholic Church." Vatican, Oct. 11, 1992. https://www.vatican.va/content/john-paul-ii/en/apost_constitutions/documents/hf_jp-ii_apc_19921011_fidei-depositum.html.
———. *On the Relationship Between Faith and Reason (Fides et Ratio)*. Translated by the Vatican. Boston: Pauline, 1998.
Jonsson, Ulf. *Foundations for Knowing God: Bernard Lonergan's Foundations for Knowledge of God and the Challenge from Antifoundationalism*. European University Studies 23. Frankfurt: Lang, 1999.
Kanaris, Jim. *Bernard Lonergan's Philosophy of Religion: From Philosophy of God to Philosophy of Religious Studies*. Albany: State University of New York Press, 2002.
Kant, Immanuel. *Critique of Pure Reason*. Translated by Norman Kemp Smith. New York: Palgrave Macmillan, 2007.

Bibliography

———. *Kritik der reinen Vernunft*. 2 vols. Frankfurt am Main: Suhrkamp, 1974.
Keller, Timothy. *The Reason for God: Belief in an Age of Skepticism*. New York: Dutton, 2008.
Kerr, Fergus. "Knowing God by Reason Alone: What Vatican I Never Said." *New Blackfriars* 91 (2010) 215–28.
Kittel, Gerhard, and Gerhard Friedrich, eds. *Theological Dictionary of the New Testament Abridged in One Volume*. Translated by Geoffrey W. Bromiley. Grand Rapids: Eerdmans, 1985.
Kleutgen, Joseph. *Die Philosophie der Vorzeit vertheidigt*. 2 vols. 2nd ed. Innsbruck: Rauch, 1878.
———. *La philosophie scolastique: Exposée et défendue*. Translated by Constant Sierp. 4 vols. Paris: Gaume Frères et Duprey, 1869.
Knox, Ronald A. *The Belief of Catholics*. New York: Harper and Brothers, 1927.
Koterski, Joseph W. *An Introduction to Medieval Philosophy: Basic Concepts*. Chichester: Wiley-Blackwell, 2009.
Lakner, Franz. "Kleutgen und die kirchliche Wissenschaft Deutschlands im 19. Jahrhundert." *ZKT* 57 (1933) 161–214.
Latourelle, René. "Absence and Presence of Fundamental Theology at Vatican II." In *Vatican II: Assessment and Perspectives; Twenty-Five Years After (1962–1987)*, edited by René Latourelle, 3:378–415. Mahwah, NJ: Paulist, 1989.
———. "Apologetics II: Nature and Task." In *Dictionary of Fundamental Theology*, edited by René Latourelle and Rino Fisichella, 35–39. English ed. edited by René Latourelle. New York: Crossroad, 1994.
———. *Theology of Revelation*. New York: Alba, 1967.
Laughland, John. *Schelling Versus Hegel: From German Idealism to Christian Metaphysics*. Aldershot, UK: Ashgate, 2007.
Lévy-Bruhl, Lucien. *La philosophie de Jacobi*. Paris: Alcan, 1894.
Liddy, Richard M. *Transforming Light: Intellectual Conversion in the Early Lonergan*. South Orange, NJ: Bernard Lonergan Institute, 2008.
Lipka, Michael. "Why America's 'Nones' Left Religion Behind." Pew Research, Aug. 24, 2016. https://www.pewresearch.org/short-reads/2016/08/24/why-americas-nones-left-religion-behind.
Lisska, Anthony J. *Aquinas's Theory of Perception: An Analytic Reconstruction*. Oxford: Oxford University Press, 2016.
———. "Right Reason in Natural Law Moral Theory." In *Reason, Religion, and Natural Law: From Plato to Spinoza*, edited by Jonathan A. Jacobs, 155–74. New York: Oxford University Press, 2012.
Livingston, James C. *Modern Christian Thought*. 2 vols. 2nd ed. Minneapolis: Fortress, 2006.
Lonergan, Bernard. "Analysis of Faith." *Method: Journal of Lonergan Studies* 20 (2002) 125–54.
———. "Cognitional Structure." In *Collection*, 205–21.
———. *Collection*. Edited by Frederick E. Crowe and Robert M. Doran. 2nd ed. Toronto: University of Toronto Press, 1988.

———. "Doctrinal Pluralism." In *Philosophical and Theological Papers, 1965-1980*, 70–104.
———. "Horizons and Transpositions." In *Philosophical and Theological Papers*, 409–31.
———. *Insight: A Study of Human Understanding*. Edited by Frederick E. Crowe and Robert M. Doran. 5th ed. Toronto: University of Toronto Press, 1992.
———. "*Insight*: Revisited." In *Second Collection*, 263–78.
———. "An Interview with Fr. Bernard Lonergan, S.J. [1970]." In *Second Collection*, 209–30.
———. *Method in Theology*. 2nd ed. Toronto: University of Toronto Press, 2003.
———. "The Natural Desire to See God." In *Collection*, 81–91.
———. "Natural Knowledge of God." In *Second Collection*, 117–33.
———. *Philosophical and Theological Papers, 1958-1964*. Edited by Robert C. Croken, Frederick E. Crowe, and Robert M. Doran. Toronto: University of Toronto Press, 1996.
———. *Philosophical and Theological Papers, 1965-1980*. Edited by Robert C. Croken and Robert M. Doran. Toronto: University of Toronto Press, 2004.
———. "Philosophical Positions with Regard to Knowing." In *Philosophical and Theological Papers, 1958-1964*, 214–43.
———. "Philosophy of God, and Theology." In *Philosophical and Theological Papers, 1965-1980*, 159–218.
———. "The Scope of Renewal." In *Philosophical and Theological Papers, 1965-1980*, 282–98.
———. *A Second Collection: Papers*. Edited by William F. J. Ryan and Bernard J. Tyrrell. Toronto: University of Toronto Press, 1996.
———. "Theology and Understanding." In *Collection*, 114–32.
———. *Understanding and Being: The Halifax Lectures on "Insight."* Edited by Elizabeth A. Murray and Mark D. Morelli. 2nd ed. Toronto: University of Toronto Press, 1990.
———. "Variations in Fundamental Theology." In *Philosophical and Theological Papers, 1965-1980*, 241–58.
———. *Verbum: Word and Idea in Aquinas*. Edited by Frederick E. Crowe and Robert M. Doran. Toronto: University of Toronto Press, 1997.
Long, Brid. "Years of Controversy." In "The Theme of Conversion in the Life and Works of Abbé Louis Bautain (1796–1867)," 122–61. PhD diss., Gregorian University, 1990.
Long, Steven A. *Natura Pura: On the Recovery of Nature in the Doctrine of Grace*. New York: Fordham University Press, 2010.
Lovejoy, Arthur O. *The Reason, the Understanding, and Time*. Baltimore: Johns Hopkins Press, 1961.
Mann, William E. "Faith and Reason." In *The Cambridge History of Medieval Philosophy*, edited by Robert Pasnau, 2:707–19. Cambridge Histories—Philosophy & Political Thought. Cambridge: Cambridge University Press, 2014.

BIBLIOGRAPHY

Mansi, Giovanni Domenico, ed. *Sacrorum Conciliorum Nova et Amplissima Collectio.* 53 vols. Arnhem: Welter, 1923–27.

Mathews, William A. *Lonergan's Quest: A Study of Desire in the Authoring of "Insight."* Toronto: University of Toronto Press, 2005.

McCool, Gerald A. *Catholic Theology in the Nineteenth Century: The Quest for a Unitary Method.* New York: Seabury, 1977.

———. *Nineteenth-Century Scholasticism: The Search for a Unitary Method.* New York: Fordham University Press, 1989.

McDermott, John M. "Faith, Reason, and Freedom." *ITQ* 67 (2002) 307–32.

McPartland, Thomas J. *Lonergan and the Philosophy of Historical Existence.* Columbia: University of Missouri Press, 2001.

Mettepenningen, Jürgen. "*Nouvelle Théologie*: Four Historical Stages of Theological Reform Towards *Ressourcement* (1935–1965)." In *"Ressourcement": A Movement for Renewal in Twentieth-Century Catholic Theology*, edited by Gabriel Flynn and Paul D. Murray, 172–84. Oxford: Oxford University Press, 2012.

Meynell, Hugo A. *An Introduction to the Philosophy of Bernard Lonergan.* 2nd ed. London: Macmillan, 1991.

———. *Redirecting Philosophy: Reflections on the Nature of Knowledge from Plato to Lonergan.* Toronto: University of Toronto Press, 1998.

Mouroux, Jean. *Je crois en Toi: Structure personnelle de la foi.* Paris: Revue des jeunes, 1949.

Newman, John Henry. *An Essay in Aid of a Grammar of Assent.* Garden City, NY: Image, 1955.

Niederbacher, Bruno. "The Relation of Reason to Faith." In *The Oxford Handbook of Aquinas*, edited by Brian Davies and Eleonore Stump, 337–47. Oxford Handbooks. New York: Oxford University Press, 2012.

Nola, Robert, and Howard Sankey. *Theories of Scientific Method: An Introduction.* Stocksfield, UK: Acumen, 2007.

O'Meara, Thomas F. *Romantic Idealism and Roman Catholicism: Schelling and the Theologians.* Notre Dame: University of Notre Dame Press, 1982.

Ott, Ludwig. *Fundamentals of Catholic Dogma.* Translated by Patrick Lynch. Fort Collins, CO: Roman Catholic, 1954.

Pottmeyer, Hermann-Josef. *Der Glaube vor dem Anspruch der Wissenschaft: Die Konstitution über den katholischen Glauben "Dei Filius" des Ersten Vatikanischen Konzils und die unveröffentlichten theologischen Voten der vorbereitenden Kommission.* Freiburg: Herder, 1968.

———. "Der Höhepunkt der Auseinandersetzung um Glauben und Wissenschaft im 19. Jahrhundert: Dogmatisch-historische Untersuchung der Konstitution 'Dei Filius' des 1. Vatikanischen Konzils." 3 vols. PhD diss., Pontifical Gregorian University, 1963.

Poupard, Paul. *Un essai de philosophie chrétienne au XIXe siècle: L'abbé Louis Bautain.* Tournai: Desclée, 1961.

Pritz, Joseph. *Glauben und Wissen bei Anton Günther.* Vienna: Herder, 1963.

Ratzinger, Joseph. "The Author of the Catechism and Its Authority." In *Introduction to the Catechism of the Catholic Church*, by Joseph Ratzinger and Christoph Schönborn, 23–27. San Francisco: Ignatius, 1994.

———. "*Dogmatic Constitution on Divine Revelation*: Chapter 1." In *Commentary on the Documents of Vatican II*, edited by Herbert Vorgrimler, 3:170–80. New York: Herder and Herder, 1967–69.

Reardon, Bernard. *Liberalism and Tradition: Aspects of Catholic Thought in Nineteenth-Century France*. Cambridge: Cambridge University Press, 1975.

———. *Religion in the Age of Romanticism*. Cambridge: Cambridge University Press, 1985.

Régny, Eugène de. *L'abbé Bautain: Sa vie et ses oeuvres*. Paris: Bray et Retaux, 1884.

Rowland, Tracey. *Catholic Theology*. Doing Theology. New York: Bloomsbury, 2017.

Ryan, Ambrose. "The Knowledge of God Attainable by Human Reason, According to the Vatican Council." *Franciscan Studies* 3 (1943) 364–73.

Sauer, James B. *A Commentary on Lonergan's "Method in Theology."* Edited by Peter L. Monette and Christine Jamieson. Ottawa: Lonergan Web Site, 2001.

Schäfer, Theo. *Die erkenntnistheoretische Kontroverse Kleutgen-Günther: Ein Beitrag zur Entstehungsgeschichte der Neuscholastik*. Paderborn: Schöningh, 1961.

Schatz, Klaus. *Vaticanum I, 1869–1870*. 3 vols. Paderborn: Schöningh, 1992–94.

Second Vatican Council. *Dogmatic Constitution on Divine Revelation (Dei Verbum)*. In *Vatican Council II: The Conciliar and Postconciliar Documents*, edited by Austin Flannery, 750–65. Rev. ed. Northport, NY: Costello, 1996.

Shanley, Brian J. *The Thomist Tradition*. Dordrecht: Kluwer, 2002.

Smith, Gregory. "About Three-in-Ten U.S. Adults Are Now Religiously Unaffiliated." Pew Research, Dec. 14, 2021. https://www.pewresearch.org/religion/2021/12/14/about-three-in-ten-u-s-adults-are-now-religiously-unaffiliated.

———. "The Changing Religious Composition of the U.S." Pew Research, May 12, 2015. Chapter 1 of *America's Changing Religious Landscape*, edited by Alan Cooperman. https://www.pewresearch.org/religion/2015/05/12/chapter-1-the-changing-religious-composition-of-the-u-s.

Smith, George D. "Faith and Revealed Truth." In *The Teaching of the Catholic Church: A Summary of Catholic Doctrine*, edited by George D. Smith, 1–37. 2nd ed. London: Burns, Oates, and Washbourne, 1952.

Spitzer, Robert J. *New Proofs for the Existence of God: Contributions of Contemporary Physics and Philosophy*. Grand Rapids: Eerdmans, 2010.

St. Amour, Paul. "On the Validity of Extrinsic Causality in Proofs for the Existence of God." *Lonergan Workshop* 21 (2008) 313–47.

Tallon, Andrew. *Head and Heart: Affection, Cognition, Volition as Triune Consciousness*. New York: Fordham University Press, 1997.

BIBLIOGRAPHY

Tanner, Norman P., ed. *Decrees of the Ecumenical Councils.* 2 vols. London: Sheed and Ward, 1990.

Tavard, George H. "Commentary on *De Revelatione.*" *JES* 3 (1966) 1–35.

Turner, Denys. *Faith, Reason, and the Existence of God.* Cambridge: Cambridge University Press, 2004.

Tyrrell, Bernard. *Bernard Lonergan's Philosophy of God.* Notre Dame: University of Notre Dame, 1974.

Vacant, Alfred. *Études théologiques sur les Constitutions du Concile du Vatican d'après les Actes du Concile.* 2 vols. Paris: Delhomme et Briguet, 1895.

Van Riet, Georges. *Thomistic Epistemology: Studies Concerning the Problem of Cognition in the Contemporary Thomistic School.* Translated by Gabriel Franks et al. 2 vols. St. Louis: Herder, 1963–65.

Vertin, Michael. "Properly Situating Philosophical Arguments for God." *Analecta Hermeneutica: Journal of the International Institute for Hermeneutics* 2 (2010). https://www.iih-hermeneutics.org/volume-2.

Vincelette, Alan. *Recent Catholic Philosophy: The Nineteenth Century.* Marquette Studies in Philosophy 58. Milwaukee: Marquette University Press, 2009.

Walter, Peter. "Die neuscholastische Philosophie im deutschsprachigen Raum." In *Christliche Philosophie im katholischen Denken des 19. und 20. Jahrhunderts,* edited by Emerich Coreth et al., 2:131–94. Graz: Styria, 1987–90.

Wenzel, Paul. *Das wissenschaftliche Anliegen des Güntherianismus: Ein Beitrag zur theologiegeschichte des 19. Jahrhunderts.* Essen: Ludgerus, 1961.

Wicks, Jared. *Doing Theology.* Mahwah, NJ: Paulist, 2009.

Wolf, Hubert. *The Nuns of Sant'Ambrogio: The True Story of a Convent in Scandal.* Translated by Ruth Martin. New York: Vintage, 2016.

Zagzebski, Linda. "A Modern Defense of Religious Authority." *Logos* 19 (2016) 15–28.

www.ingramcontent.com/pod-product-compliance
Lightning Source LLC
Chambersburg PA
CBHW072156160426
43197CB00012B/2403